Bicycling in New Jersey 30 Tours

Bicycling in New Jersey 30 Tours

by

Harold L. Poor

ENSLOW PUBLISHERS
Bloy Street and Ramsey Avenue
Box 777
Hillside, New Jersey 07205

I would like to thank my friend Tom Kersch for accompanying me on many of these tours and for typing the entire manuscript. This book is dedicated to him and to my children, Liz and Chris, with the hope that they will find it a source of pleasure in the future.

Library of Congress Cataloging in Publication Data

Poor, Harold L
  Bicycling in New Jersey.

  1. Cycling—New Jersey—Guide-books. 2. Cycling paths—New Jersey—Guide-books. 3. New Jersey—Description and travel—1951- —Guide-books.
I. Title.

GV1045.5.N5P66   917.49′04′4   78-1996
ISBN 0-89490-013-7

Manufactured in the United States of America

10   9   8   7   6   5   4   3

TABLE OF CONTENTS

NEW JERSEY

INTRODUCTION: WHAT TO EXPECT FROM THIS BOOK AND OTHER INFORMATION

Many people whose acquaintance with New Jersey is limited to the turnpike think of the state solely as an industrial corridor between Philadelphia and New York City. In actuality, New Jersey contains beautiful, rolling countryside, unpopulated beaches, magnificent mountains and valleys, and thousands of miles of little used roads. From the plains in the south to the mountains in the north, New Jersey offers ample opportunities for cyclists whatever their abilities. Beginners will find the shore and area south of Princeton suitable for their needs, while expert riders will discover that the steep trails of the region around High Point offer a challenge to their skill and stamina.

New Jersey is the most heavily urbanized and industrialized state in the nation. Yet, much of its rural character has been retained, confirmed by the fact that New Jersey is second only to Florida and California in the production of fresh fruit and vegetables. Even the bleakest cities lie close to beautiful, natural landscapes. There are the mysterious pine barrens; the open, sandy beaches (unlike other coastal states, virtually the whole of the Jersey shore is open to the public); the exotic Great Swamp, and the beautiful Delaware Water Gap in the northern mountains.

In addition, New Jersey is rich in places of historical interest. The number of houses George Washington slept in during the revolutionary campaigns is matched only by the number of "headquarters" he established. In other words, the state abounds in colonial architecture, battlefields of the revolution, and other historic sites important in the early history of this country. Most are carefully preserved or have been meticulously restored.

This book assumes that you own a ten-speed bicycle and know the rudiments of its operation and repair. If you are just beginning and need advice about selecting a bicycle suitable for your needs or if you want to read more about riding techniques and rules of safety, there are a large number of books about these subjects on the market. Two of the best are Delong's Guide to Bicycles by Fred Delong (Chilton, 1974) and the New Complete Book of Bicycling by Eugene A. Sloan (Simon and Schuster, 1974). Excellent advice about all aspects of cycling regularly appears in Bicycling! magazine. The organization that looks out for the interests of cyclists and forms their legislative lobby in Washington is the League of American Wheelmen which publishes the excellent L.A.W. Bulletin. The Bulletin, in addition to information on all aspects of bicycling, regularly lists events, races, and rides throughout the country.

Many of the tours assume that you will arrive by automobile early in the morning and spend the day cycling. Yet, a substantial number of points of departure may be reached by public transportation that welcomes both you and your bicycle. From New York City, you can take the PATH train to Newark, but you will need a special permit for your bike (see Tour 18). Also from New York City, the Suburban Transit Company buses, that run to New Brunswick and Princeton, will transport bikes in the luggage compartment if there is room (see Part I and Part II). In addition, there are buses from the George Washington Bridge terminal to Paterson. The trips are designed to be interlocking so that in theory, once in New Jersey, a cyclist could follow their directions and pedal around the entire state without any assistance whatsoever from an internal combustion engine.

Maps are expensive and most tour books provide only a rudimentary outline. In contrast, we have provided enough detail so that you may find your way back to the course if you get lost. And the maps are designed to enable you to work out short-cuts or alternatives to the routes proposed. However, a word of caution is also in order. The maps are intended to be used along with the carefully detailed directions. The maps are not drawn to scale and may not be used to judge distances. It is therefore not advisable to ignore the instructions and try to use the maps alone. If you feel insecure with the maps, you may purchase county maps. The Hagstrom company produces good ones and you may purchase them directly by writing The Hagstrom Company, Inc., 450 West 33rd Street, New York, New York, 10001. The average price of each map is around $2.00. In addition, many of the individual counties of New Jersey publish their own maps, which are either free or available at nominal cost. You may obtain information by writing or calling the individual county seat. The maps vary in quality. Hunterdon County, for example has produced an excellent map, which may be bought in the courthouse in Flemington for $1.00.

The instructions for each tour give the maximum round-trip distance, the condition of the course, and the minimum time required to travel it. Conditions are divided into "flat," "mostly flat," "rolling hills," "hilly," and "steep." For the latter, I advise a rear cluster with a cog of 28 to 32 teeth. All such tours are found only in Warren and Sussex counties--the most beautiful area of New Jersey, but also the most difficult for the cyclist. Some riders are obviously faster than others, but the minimum travel time is based on an assumption of an average speed of 10 miles per hour with brief rest stops. You best know your own abilities. Select your tour and your pace accordingly. If you are a beginner, avoid the more diffi-cult tours until you build up stamina. If you cycle regularly, you may be surprised at how rapidly you will be able to tackle the more strenuous sections of the state. It is usually also more fun to cycle with a friend and it is also safer in case of emergencies.

Especially interesting places are noted in the instructions by numbers in parentheses. These correspond to the numbers in the list at the end of each tour entitled "Places of Special Interest." These include historic sites, noted views and vistas, and suggestions for places to eat and stay. Most of the tours abound with inter-esting and beautiful things to see and do, so only the most special have been included.

Some cyclists may wonder why there are no tours in the Peapack-Gladstone area in Somerset County. The reason is simple-- the back roads are almost all unpaved and many of them are "private." Apparently gentlemen farmers prefer unpaved roads for their rural feeling, while the chief interest of genuine farmers is to get their produce to market.

The directions have been carefully checked for accuracy, but errors may have crept in. If you find that something is unclear or in error or if you have a suggestion for a tour to be included in later editions, please write to me in care of my publisher.

Tips on Equipment and Riding Techniques

1. Be sure your seat is high enough. Your leg should be almost straight when the pedal is at its lowest point.

2. Keep the balls of your feet on the pedals. To help accomplish this correct riding position, use toe clips; they allow you almost to double your efficiency. You may eventually want riding shoes with cleats, but there are now a number of good, cleatless touring shoes on the market. Don't ride in sneakers, however, since the soles are too soft and soon become uncomfortable.

3. Cycling shorts with a chamois lining are recommended, as are cycling gloves--expecially for long-distance rides. Avoid jeans since the seams can be irritating.

4. Shift to a lower gear at the bottom of hills, not in the middle. Even on flat land, use a lower gear rather than straining in a higher one. It is easier on the knees and tendons.

5. Attach a water bottle to your bike and take along fruit and candy bars for energy. Eat before you are hungry and rest before you are exhausted.

6. Take along a small wrench, screw driver, knife, rag, and appropriate tire-repair equipment. All this equipment will be useful at some point or other.

7. In summer, always wear a shirt to avoid dehydration. In colder weather, put on several layers that can be removed one by one as you warm up.

8. Do not wear a backpack. Carry all heavy gear on your bike not on yourself.

Safety

1. Always ride on the right except on one-way streets, where you may ride on the left to avoid buses.

2. Give signals when you turn or stop.

3. When making a left turn, stop on the right-hand side of the street, dismount, and walk the bike across as if you were a pedestrian.

4. Give automobiles and pedestrians the right of way.

5. Obey all traffic rules--stopping at stop lights and signs.

6. In New Jersey, you are not required to ride on the shoulder, but the law does state that you should ride as far to the right as is safe and practicable. Cyclists are not allowed to

ride on interstate highways in New Jersey, or on the New Jersey Turnpike or on the Garden State Parkway.

7. When riding with others, ride single file and indicate holes and loose gravel to a rider behind you by pointing your arm and hand stright down behind you.

8. Avoid riding at night; but if you must do so, use a light and reflectors. A reflective vest, available at most bike shops, is also recommended.

9. In the city, be on the lookout for doors on parked cars suddenly opening, and for potholes and sewer grates, which may trap your wheels. In the country, watch for soft shoulders and patches of gravel and sand. Be on the alert everywhere for glass.

10. Dogs detest bicycles. If you have the discipline and courage, the recommended procedure when chased by a dog is to dismount and stand very still. The dog is supposed to lose interest and go away. Some people carry a spray can of dog repellent.

11. In the city, some people carry police whistles, to make their presence known. Others just yell. There are compressed air horns available that can be heard for miles, but we have enough noise already without cyclists adding to the din.

Information About New Jersey

New Jersey has many state parks, forests, and recreation areas and publishes information about them. Several parks and forests have cabins that you may reserve in advance, but you must write to the administration of the individual park or forest. A free central publication lists the names, locations, addresses, and types of facilities of all the parks, forests and areas. It is entitled <u>Year Round Guide to New Jersey State Forests, Parks, Recreation Areas, Natural Areas, and Historic Sites</u> and may be obtained by writing to the Bureau of Parks, P.O. Box 1420, Trenton, New Jersey 08625.

New Jersey also has an active program for promoting cycling. Bikeways are being constructed around the state. If you have any question concerning cycling, or wish to know about cycling clubs, touring, and racing activities in your area, get in touch with The Bikeway Coordinator, State of New Jersey Department of Transportation, 1035 Parkway Avenue, Trenton, New Jersey, 08625.

A Note of Warning About Street Signs

A favorite pastime in the New Jersey and Pennsylvania area seems to be the reversing of street signs. Who or what mysterious force is responsible I have no idea, but once reversed, no sign seems ever to be put right again. So, if the sign does not agree with the map, or the road just feels funny, check and make sure the road is actually the one the sign says it is.

And finally--have fun cycling in New Jersey.

PART I: THE RUTGERS-NEW BRUNSWICK AREA

New Brunswick, the home of Rutgers University, is the gateway to rural New Jersey. The region north of New Brunswick is one of the most densely populated in the nation, but to the south and west are small towns, villages, and farms. To the east, of course, is the ocean, surprisingly accessible for the Rutgers-New Brunswick cyclist.

There are six tours in all from Rutgers. In addition to exploring the immediate area around New Brunswick-Piscataway, two of the trips lead to the beach, one to Hunterdon County, another to the fields and farms around Cranbury and, of course, the necessary tour to Princeton via the historic Griggstown Canal route. All together, the trips form a kind of representative example of New Jersey cycling--the flat area around Englishtown, the canals and waterways near Princeton and the hills surrounding Flemington.

New Brunswick is approximately 30 miles from New York City and may be reached by both train and bus. During non-rush hours, you may take your bike on the bus, storing it in the luggage compartment. However, much depends on the whim of the driver. If he refuses to let you take your bike, there is not much you can do except wait for the next bus and hope for a more understanding driver. In general, I have found bus personnel to be courteous and helpful. Suburban Transit Company buses leave for New Brunswick from the Port Authority bus terminal in New York City every half-hour during the day and the same is true for the return to New York.

16

All of the tours from Rutgers leave from the Old Queens building on Hamilton Street. However, if you come by car, you may park in the Sears parking lot at the conjunction of Routes 1 and 18. Ryder's Lane, which you take to the shore and to Englishtown is to the left as you face away from the rear of Sears. To get to Hamilton Street for the other tours, facing away from the rear of Sears, go left onto Clifton Avenue, left onto George Street which passes through the Douglass College campus. Continue through New Brunswick to Rutgers College and then turn left onto Hamilton Street.

Tour 1: Rutgers to Princeton

The tour links the two collegiate rivals that are New Jersey's foremost institutions of higher learning. Both Rutgers and Princeton universities began as colonial colleges. After World War II, Rutgers became the state university of New Jersey and has expanded to encompass four undergraduate colleges and numerous professional schools with branches in both Newark and Camden. Princeton remained private and became an outstanding member of the Ivy League. For over 200 years, the two colleges have been scholastic and athletic competitors. They played the first intercollegiate football game in 1869, the year from which the game officially dates its beginning. The tour begins at Old Queens, the oldest building of Rutgers College and extends to Nassau Hall, Princeton's oldest building. It runs through fields, meadows and working farms, and extends along the Griggstown portion of the historic Delaware-Raritan Canal. The route is surprisingly rural in spite of its proximity to urban centers and major highways-- all of which are studiously avoided. You may shorten this trip by 10 miles or so by retracing your trip back to Griggstown from Princeton.

Maximum round trip distance: 50 miles
Course: Mostly flat with a few hills
Minimum travel time: 5 hours

Directions:

Facing away from Old Queens (1)
go left on Hamilton Street, follow Hamilton for approximately 5 miles to Middlebush where a stone church with a bright red door is in the middle of the intersection of three roads

18

Go to the right of the church on the continuation of Hamilton Street, which has become Amwell Road, (County Route 514), follow Amwell Road to East Millstone (If you cross the bridge over the canal into Millstone, you have gone too far)

Left onto Market Street in East Millstone (2)

Right onto Elm Street which bears immediately left and becomes Canal Road--which runs along the historic Griggstown Canal (3) (a bit of gravel here and there, but not of significance)

Left at Suydam Road and immediately right again onto the continuation of Canal Road (you will see the Franklin Township Water Filtration Plant on your right)

Stop at Griggstown General Store (4) for a rest if desired.

Right at the end of Canal Road onto Washington Street (County Route 518) into Rocky Hill (5)

Left onto Princeton Avenue at the Rocky Hill Inn

Bear left at the fork onto Mt. Lucas Road

Follow across all intersections into Witherspoon Street, which leads you to the main gate of Princeton University and Nassau Hall (6)

To return to Rutgers:

Facing away from the main gate, left onto Nassau Street (Route 27 north)

Bear left onto Stockton Street in direction of Lawrenceville-Trenton

Right onto Elm Road (direction of Hopewell), which becomes Great Road

Follow Great Road which crosses County Route 518 and becomes County Route 113, the Belle-Meade-Blawenburg Road (there are many sharp curves)

Right onto the Dutchtown-Harlingen Road

Cross Route 206 onto the continuation of Harlingen Road

Bear left at the Maple Street fork to continue on course on Harlingen Road (gravel for 2/10 mile)

Left onto continuation of Harlingen Road at the intersection of Harlingen and Mill Pond Roads

Right onto the Belle-Meade-Griggstown Road, unmarked

Left onto River Road, (County Route 533)

Immediate right onto Griggstown Causeway and follow back to Griggstown General Store

Left onto Canal Road

Right onto Suydam Road

Left onto South Middlebush Road, unmarked (at the end of Suydam Road)

Right onto Hamilton Street and return to Rutgers

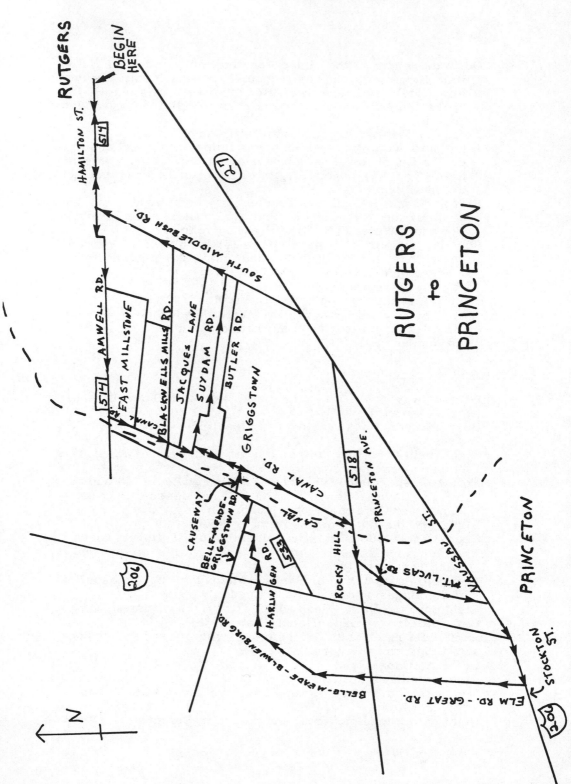

RUTGERS to PRINCETON

Places of Special Interest

1. Old Queens, original building of Rutgers College, founded in 1766 and known as Queens College until after the Revolution. You might wish to turn right on College Avenue and visit Buccleuch Mansion in Buccleuch Park. The mansion is now a museum and for a time served as British Headquarters during the Revolution. It appears to be one of the few historic houses in the area in which Washington did not sleep.

2. Chester and Sons Groceries in East Millstone--make excellent sandwiches. The large elm in front of the church to the left on Elm Street provides excellent shade for a picnic.

3. Griggstown Canal portion of the Delaware-Raritan Canal system, which was in continuous use from colonial times almost to the present and is now designated a historic landmark. Canal Road forms part of the route that Washington took to New York after the Battle of Trenton.

4. Griggstown General Store on Griggstown Causeway--a good place for sandwiches, ice cream, and other refreshments, which are best consumed overlooking the canal from the bridge. You may see townsfolk swimming--sometimes with their horses. There are often other cyclists there, too.

5. Rocky Hill, another colonial town. If you continue up Washington Street, you will see on your left a fine old carpenter gothic church, an excellent example of its kind.

6. Nassau Hall built in 1756. Princeton University founded in 1747 is located in one of the most beautiful towns of New Jersey. Princeton's Nassau Street is rich in shops, restaurants and delicatessens.

Tour 2: Rutgers-Piscataway

A tour designed primarily for residents of the New Brunswick area who want a quick work out without having to ride far from home. This means some traffic, a few suburban streets, and a glimpse of industrial ugliness. But the major portion of the tour passes through Johnson Park along the Raritan River, the beautiful Busch Campus of Rutgers University, the grounds of Livingston College (also Rutgers), and beside working farms and cultivated fields. There are also several cemeteries or "memorial parks," as they style themselves, and they add to the serenity of the route.

Maximum round-trip distance: 20 miles
Course: mostly flat
Minimum travel time: 2 hours

Directions:

> Facing away from Old Queens, right onto Hamilton Street
> Left onto George Street
> Right onto the Landing Lane Bridge and cross the Raritan River
> Left onto the park drive through Johnson Park (just before busy River Road, Route 18) you will see the bird sanctuary to your left
> Continue through the park, you will see "Olde Towne"--a reconstructed colonial village--on your right and the head quarters of the Middlesex County park police on your left.
> At the traffic light, cross River Road (Route 18) onto Hoes Lane
> Left at the stop sign onto the continuation of Hoes Lane, which has now become a four-lane divided highway
> Left onto Park Avenue
> Right onto Witherspoon Street, which becomes Custer Street
> Left onto Plainfield Avenue
> Right at the stop sign beside the Sunoco station onto River Road (Route 18), careful here as traffic can be heavy
> Cross Interstate 287
> Right onto Haywood Avenue (second right after I-287)

22

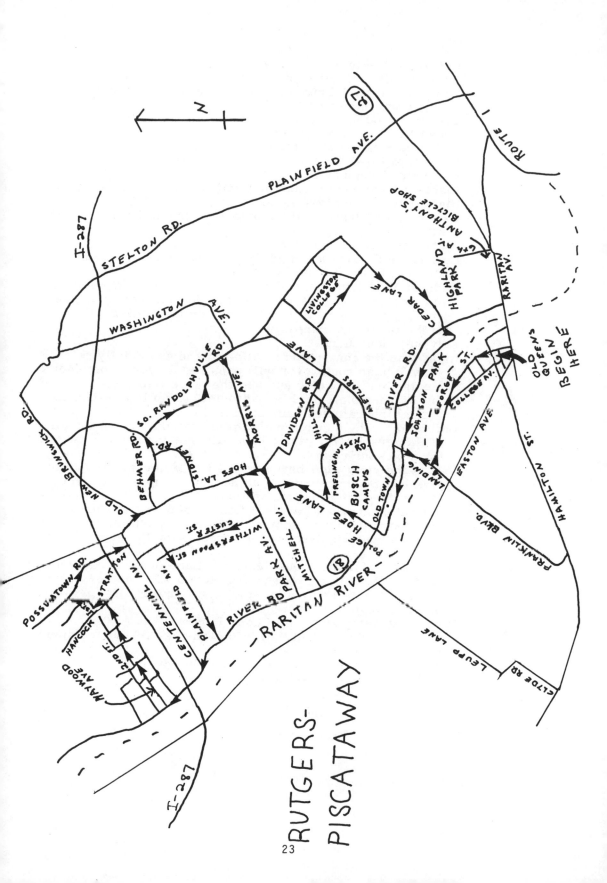

RUTGERS-
PISCATAWAY

Left onto Crestwood Street and

Immediately right onto 2nd Avenue

Cross Brentwood Drive onto the continuation of 2nd Avenue (right and immediately left)

Cross Elwood Street onto the continuation of 2nd Avenue

Cross Hancock Road and go

Left onto Stratton Street South

Right onto First Avenue

Left onto Normandy Drive

Right onto the continuation of First Avenue

Right onto Possumtown Road

Left at the traffic light onto Centennial Avenue (a busy street)

Right onto Hoes Lane

Left at the Piscataway High School onto Behmer Road

Right onto South Randolphville Road

Right at the first intersection (not counting the cemetery entrance) onto unmarked Morris Avenue (you will see a small white concrete block house on the corner belonging to the telephone company)

Left onto Hoes Lane

Right onto the continuation of Hoes Lane and briefly retrace your former route. You will pass the Rutgers Community Mental Health Center and see the large Georgian tower of the Rutgers biological laboratories. Just beyond the biological laboratories parking lot

Left onto Freuylinghuysen Road through the Busch Campus of Rutgers University. You will see the university golf links on your right

Left at the yield sign beyond the Hill Center for the Mathematical Sciences onto an unmarked campus road and go to the third intersection

Right onto unmarked Davidson Road. You will see the large glass and steel administration services building of Rutgers on your right-known by students as the crystal palace.

At the traffic light, cross Metlar's Lane in the direction of Livingston College whose campus you will see before you

Right at the intersection at the sign saying of "physical plant, design and construction"

Right at the stop sign onto Cedar Lane

Cross River Road (Route 18) into Johnson Park and continue through the park

Left onto Landing Lane and recross the river

Left onto George Street and return to your starting point.

Tour 3: Rutgers-Englishtown-Cranbury

A tour through the mid-Jersey countryside to Englishtown, site of the noted weekend flea market. The terrain is generally flat and can be negotiated with little effort even by beginning cyclists. If you begin early enough, you may want to ride the tour entitled "In and Around Englishtown" which can be found at the end of this section.

Maximum round-trip distance: 60 miles
Course: mostly flat
Minimum travel time: 7 hours

Directions:

> Facing away from Old Queens right onto Hamilton Street
> Right onto George Street
> Right onto Clifton Avenue after you pass Douglass College
> Right onto Ryders Lane--you will see the Sears parking lot directly ahead before you turn (people who have come by car begin here)
> Right onto Dunham's Corner Road
> Cross Cranbury Road onto Helmetta Boulevard
> Right onto Lake Avenue, which becomes Maple Street
> Left onto Main Street in Helmetta
> Right onto Devoe Avenue in Spotswood, which becomes the Spotswood-Englishtown Road
> Left onto Wood Avenue (County Route 522), which becomes Water Street in Englishtown (1)

To return to Rutgers-New Brunswick:

> Return to Water Street
> Bear left at the fork onto LaSatta Avenue, which becomes Tracy Station Road
> Contiue straight ahead onto Federal Road
> Cross Perrineville Road, continuing on Federal Road
> Right at the stop sign onto Union Valley-Applegarth Road
> Left onto Union Valley Road in the direction of Cranbury
> Right onto Applegarth Road
> Left onto Cranbury-Half Acre Road
> Cross Route 130 in the direction of Cranbury
> Left onto County Route 535, Maplewood Avenue in Cranbury (2)

25

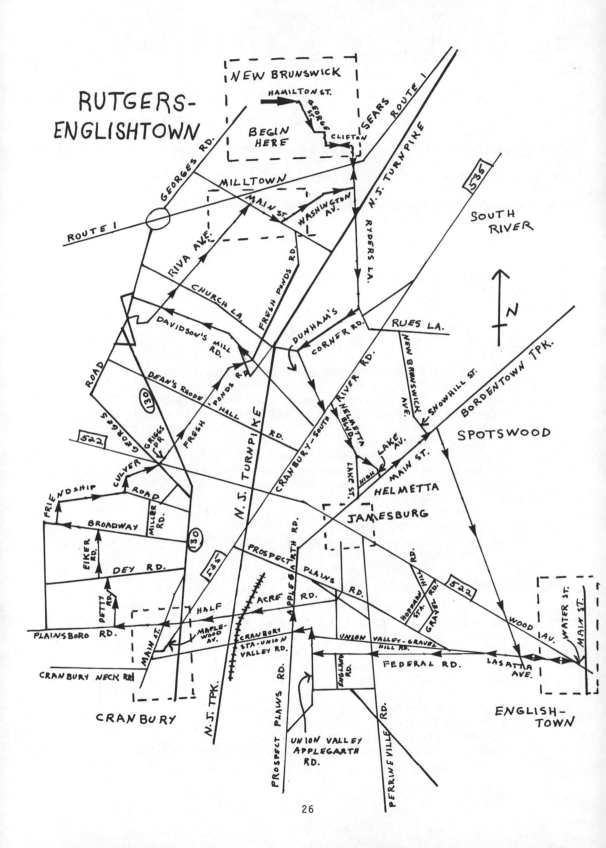

RUTGERS-ENGLISHTOWN

Right onto the Plainsboro Road

Cross Main Street and continue on the Plainsboro Road

Right onto Petty Road

Left at the stop sign onto unmarked Dey Road

Immediate right onto Eiker Road

Left at the intersection onto unmarked Broadway

First right onto Friendship Road

Left onto Culver Road

Cross the intersection in the direction of Jamesburg-Englishtown

Left onto Griggs Drive

Cross Route 130 to the continuation of Griggs Drive, which is Fresh Ponds Road

Left onto Davidson's Mills Road

Right onto Riva Avenue (if you wish to see the lovely Old Mill Pond and waterfall, turn left onto Riva Avenue and go for about a half mile until you see the pond and waterfall. Then retrace your route and continue straight ahead on Riva Avenue across Davidson's Mill Road.) Riva Avenue continues along the millstream past Lake Farrington into Milltown

Right onto Main Street in Milltown

Left onto Washington Avenue

Left onto Ryder's Lane, which leads you back to your starting place in New Brunswick

Places of Special Interest

1. Englishtown--To get to the flea market on weekends, left onto Main Street and bear left at the Exxon station. A good place in Englishtown to rest and have a sandwich is at "Joe's," as it is sometimes called--you can recognize it by the faded neon sign at front saying "Fountain-Service"--just off Water Street to the right on Main Street.

2. Cranbury-- Charming colonial and early 19th century town with a lovely pond in its middle in which children still swim in the summer. Behind the Cranbury Inn is the Cranbury Historical and Preservation Society Museum, which has furniture and costumes from the early 19th Century. Opposite the Cranbury Inn is the First Presbyterian Church built in 1734 and a fine example of Colonial church architecture.

Tour 4: Rutgers to Flemington

A longish tour through the beautiful countryside of Hunterdon County. Quickly leaving the urban congestion of New Brunswick behind, the route leads through charming villages and towns such as Neshanic and Zion to Flemington with its beautiful court house and other examples of colonial architecture. Unlike the other tours in Hunterdon County, the course is easy in general with only a few real hills. Still, its length requires stamina, so judge yourself accordingly.

Maximum round-trip distance: 65 miles
Course: rolling hills, some steep
Minimum travel time: 8 hours

Directions:

Facing away from Old Queens, go left on Hamilton Street in the direction of Somerset

Cross College Avenue and continue on Hamilton Street (which is County Route 514)

Follow Route 514 through Middlebush with its fine stone church in the middle of an intersection (you bear right at the church). Beyond Middlebush, 514 is called Amwell Road. You will pass the Rutgers Forest, Metlar's Woods, on your left and the entrance to Colonial Park (1) on your right. Continue to follow Route 514/Amwell Road on its curving course

Cross the Raritan Canal into Millstone

Left onto County Route 533 and

Immediately right onto the continuation of Route 514/Amwell Road to remain on course

Cross Route 206, continuing on 514. You can get provisions at the large A & P on your left--unfortunately there are a few miles of suburban sprawl here.

Left onto the continuation of 514/Amwell Road at the Hillsboro General Store/Jack's Service Station in the direction of Neshanic (this is easy to miss, so be alert)

Proceed into the small town of Neshanic (2)

Left onto Zion Road just past the church in Neshanic (up hill here)

28

Left at the stop sign onto Long Hill Road (there is one mile of light gravel here--if you have very delicate tires, you may want to walk. I think, however, the beauty of the spot is worth the inconvenience.)

Continue straight ahead through all intersections into the village of Zion and onto the Zion- Wertsville Road in the direction of Wertsville

Right onto Lindbergh Road

Left at the end of Lindbergh Road onto County Route 602 (Wertsville Road)

Right (almost immediately) onto Manners Road (County Route 609) in the direction of Reaville--note the beautiful farms and fields here.

Left onto Amwell Road/514 in the direction of Ringoes

Immediate right onto the 514 spur in the direction of Flemington and Three Bridges

Left at the sign for Flemington onto the continuation of the 514 spur

Cross Route 202

Cross Route 31 and proceed straight ahead into Flemington (3)

Right onto Main Street

Bear right at the Gettysburg monument and Presbyterian Church in the direction of County Route 523

Cross Route 31 onto Route 523 in the direction of Whitehouse

Right at the stop sign onto River Road

Left over the bridge crossing the South Branch of the Raritan River onto Rockafellows Mills Road

Right onto Barley Sheaf Road, which resembles an English country lane

At the intersection with Locust Road or Lazy Brook Road, be sure to continue straight ahead to remain on Barley Sheaf Road

Right onto County Route 629 (Pleasant Run) at the end of Barley Sheaf Road

Cross Route 202 in the direction of Neshanic and continue on Pleasant Run crossing all intersections. Note the beautiful corn fields and mountain views here. Proceed into the town of Neshanic Station

Left onto Maple Avenue in Neshanic Station and cross the iron bridge

Right immediately after crossing the bridge onto Main Road in the direction of Neshanic (up hill here)

Left onto Amwell Road in Neshanic and

Retrace your route back to New Brunswick remaining on County Road 514 all the way to Hamilton Street.

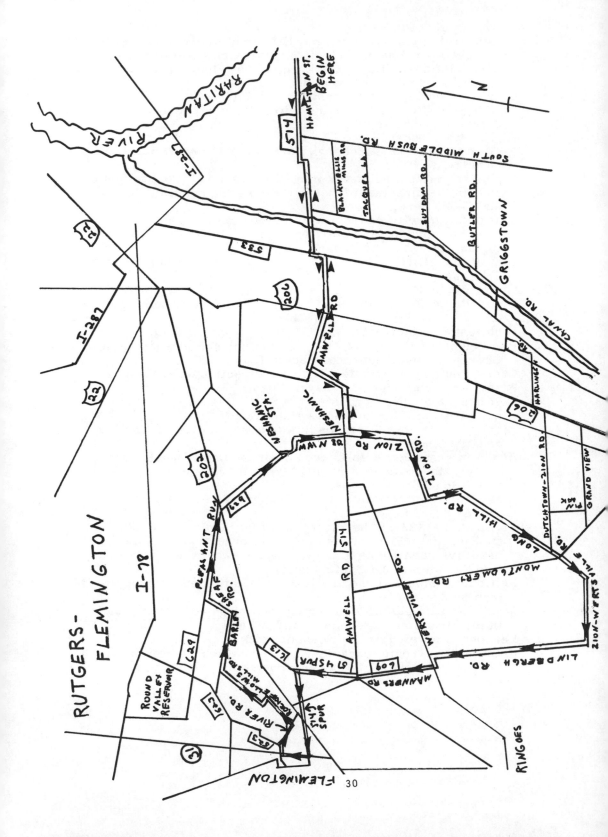

Places of Special Interest

1. Colonial Park--picnic facilities, children's playground, nature walks and bicycle paths, a good place to rest.

2. Neshanic- originally a colonial settlement with a church dating from 1752.

3. Flemington- seat of Hunterdon County, settled in 1730. Note the many interesting shops and restaurants. The beautiful courthouse, built in 1828, was the site of the famous Lindbergh kidnapping trial in 1935. Beside the courthouse is the exquisite Greek revival law office, which resembles a large, elegant doll house. The near-by Flemington glass works is also worth a visit if you have the time. In the county offices in the courthouse, a good-and inexpensive-map of Hunterdon County is available. The charge was $1.00 in the summer of 1977. Inexpensive sandwiches and other provisions may be purchased at the Court Deli next to the Greek revival law office on Main Street.

Tour 1: Rutgers To Sandy Hook

The Gateway National Park on Sandy Hook is the closest beach to central and northern New Jersey that has been preserved in its natural state. It is surrounded by industry, dense population, and busy expressways. Therefore, the tour, however much it may avoid main traffic arteries, is not always the most beautiful. Back roads sometimes run beside factories and plants or through the detritus of urban culture in the form of shopping centers, fast food places and "nite spots." But the sea and the natural beaches of Sandy Hook are worth it. While the trip to Manasquan is far more beautiful, it is also longer. The Sandy Hook tour is thus intended for Rutgers students and residents of the greater New Brunswick area who would like to spend a day at the beach with minimum cycling. A person leaving at seven in the morning in the summer can be on the beach by ten and home by seven--well before dark--if she or he departs at four. This is one of the few tours in which going and return routes are identical, but an over-night trip can be worked out in combination with the Manasquan Tour.

Maximum round-trip distance: 60 miles
Course: Mostly flat except for one long hill near the
         coast before descending to the beach.
Minimum travel time: 6 hours

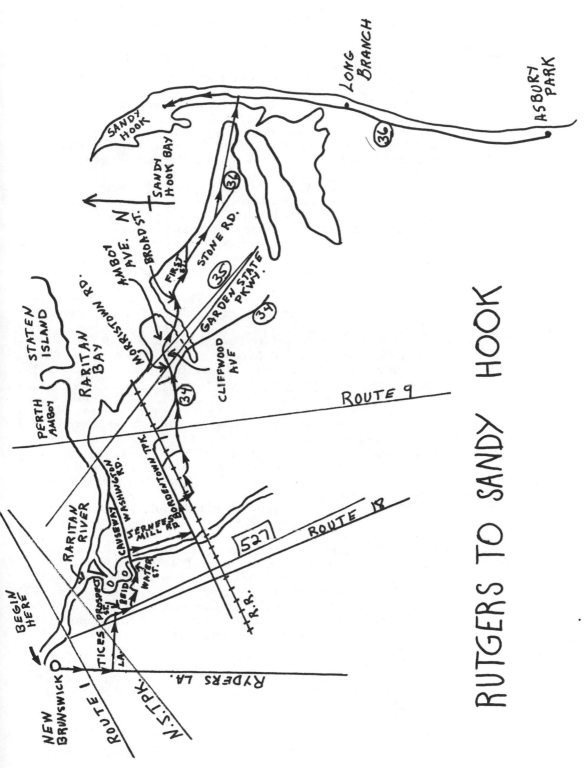

RUTGERS TO SANDY HOOK

33

Directions:

Facing away from Old Queens, right onto Hamilton Street

Right onto George Street

Right onto Clifton Avenue after passing through the Douglass College Campus (1)

Right onto Ryders Lane--people who park in the Sears lot will begin here. After crossing the New Jersey Turnpike overpass, notice the entrance to Helyar Woods (2) on your left.

Left onto Tices Lane (the street to the right reads Washington Avenue, a continuation of Tices Lane)

Right onto Route 18 (only 100 feet or so)

Right onto jughandle at sign saying Prospect Street (you are in effect making a left turn onto Prospect Street)
Cross Route 18 and continue on Prospect Street

Follow Prospect Street into Reid Street in South River to stay on course

Left onto Main Street (County Road 535) direction Sayreville

Right (immediately after crossing causeway) onto Jernees Mill Road

Left onto Bordentown-Amboy Turnpike (unmarked)

Right at first small road across railroad tracks--this is easy to miss, so be alert--if you come to the railroad underpass, you have gone too far

Left onto paved road--this is a rather ugly industrial back area, but necessary to avoid heavy traffic. Bear right at fork in road. Cross Route 9 at traffic light. Right in direction of Matawan onto Route 34. (Uphill here. Also, heavy traffic, but a wide shoulder)

Left onto Morristown Road following signs to Garden State Parkway (on county maps Morristown Road is named Cheesequake Road)

Stop, if desired, at Cheesequake State Park (3)

Continue on Morristown Road (following signs to Garden State Parkway)

At the traffic light, continue straight ahead on course (ignoring Garden State Parkway) onto Cliffwood Avenue

Cross Route 35, right at "one-way, do not enter" sign onto Amboy Avenue (bikes can sometimes do what is forbidden to autos, but be careful.) Amboy Avenue becomes South Amboy Road which becomes Front Street in Keyport (4)

Left at the four-way-stop onto Broad Street

Right onto First Street

Bear right at the fork onto Stone Road

Left onto Route 36 East for the twelve remaining miles to the entrance to Sandy Hook Gateway National Recreation Area (5).

Places of Special Interest

1. Douglass College, one of the four undergraduate colleges which make up Rutgers University. It is limited to women and for years was known as the "female half" of Rutgers before Rutgers College became coeducational.

2. Helyar Woods maintained by Cook College of Rutgers University. You might want to stop to enjoy the nature trail in the woods and the lovely views of the Weston Mill Pond.

3. Cheesequake State Park--fine stop for a rest and picnic, but you must leave the way you enter. Admission is free to cyclists.

4. Keyport--first view of the water. At last a feeling of shore. Keyport has a number of restaurants, which you might want to try, the only ones worth mention on the tour.

5. Gateway National Recreation area-Sandy Hook Unit has beautiful, unspoiled beaches and dunes. There are conducted tours of the nature walks; ask the ranger about tour times.

Tour 6: Rutgers to the Shore at Manasquan

A tour on back roads through wooded areas to the shore-- further than Sandy Hook, but far more beautiful and interesting to ride. The return is through the cultivated fields near Englishtown, an area that appears isolated and virtually devoid of inhabitants. The trip begins in front of Old Queens at Rutgers and proceeds to Manasquan via Englishtown. To get to Englishtown, follow the directions in the Rutger's-Englishtown tour.

This is a longer tour than most in this book and you may want to make it an overnighter. If so, you may desire to ride the shore route down to Island Beach State Park next door to Seaside Heights. Unforunately, there is no camping in the park and accomodations in the season may be difficult to find. However, Island Beach State Park with its sand dunes, unspoiled beaches, and almost total lack of "development" is a welcome contrast to the generally cluttered Jersey shore. It may be favorably compared to Cape Cod, Fire Island, and other shore areas considered to be natural and unspoiled. You may also combine this tour with the Sandy Hook section to create a trip of several days' duration. From Sandy Hook, you simply follow the road along the beach down to Manasquan or Island Beach and then follow the directions for the return from Manasquan to New Brunswick.

Maximum round-trip distance: 100 miles
Course: mostly flat
Minimum travel time: 12 hours

Directions:

>In Englishtown (1)
>Right onto Main Street
>Left onto Tennent Avenue in the direction of Freehold (2)
>   you will enter Freehold on Throckmorton Street--cont-
>   inue on it, cross Broad Street, the railroad tracks and
>   West Main Street--then
>Right onto South Street
>Go under the big Route 33 overpass and take your
>Immediate left onto Willowbrook Road (if you find yourself
>   suddenly on busy Route 9, you have gone too far)
>Right onto Hall's Mill Road
>Left onto the Elton Adelphia Road (see map #2)
>Right onto Havens Bridge road
>Bear left onto Casino Drive
>Cross West Farms Road
>Left onto Peskin Road, which becomes Southard Avenue
>Right onto Manassa Road
>Left onto Old Tavern Road
>Cross County Route 547 onto the Herbertsville Road (which
>is a continuation of Old Tavern Road)
>Bear left onto the Allenwood-Squankum Road (County Route
>   21)
>Left onto Hospital Road
>Right onto Atlantic Avenue (3)
>When Atlantic Avenue bears left, continue straight ahead
>onto Ramshorn Drive
>Here you will see the beginning of the bikeway, on your
>   left leading to Manasquan
>At the end of the bikeway
>Right onto the street and follow it around to the left onto
>   Main Street
>Follow Main Street to the beach

To return to Rutgers-New Brunswick:

>Return to the bikeway via Main Street
>At the end of the bikeway, go north on Atlantic Avenue
>Left onto Hospital Road
>Cross County Route 21 onto unmarked Easy Street--the
>   continuation of Hospital Road
>Cross two more intersections and follow Easy Street to its
>   end

Right onto County Route 547-- the Lakewood-Farmingdale Road

Left onto the Oak Glen-Maxim Road

Right onto Preventorium Road

Left onto Old Tavern Road

Right onto Aldrich Road

At the fork, bear right (really straight ahead) onto unmarked Windeler Road

Right onto Georgia Tavern Road just past the Land O'Pines School

Left onto Lemon Road

Left onto West Farms Road (see map #1)

Cross Route 9 onto the continuation of West Farms Road which becomes Georgia Road (4)

Cross busy Jackson Mill Road
   Left onto the Elton-Adelphia Road (County Route 524)

Right onto Thompson's Grove Road

Cross Route 537 onto the continuation of Thompson's Grove Road

Bear left onto Mill Road

Left onto Oakland Mills Road

Right at the end of Oakland Mills Road and cross the inter-section onto Alternate 527 which becomes Woodville Road

Cross Route 33 to the continuation of Woodville Road which is now called Iron Ore Road

Right at the stop sign

Left onto Jurgelsky Road

Bear left onto Dey Grove Road

Right onto the Jamesburg-Perrineville Road

Left onto Federal road

Follow instructions for return to New Brunswick in the Rutgers-Englishtown-Cranbury tour-beginning with Federal Road on the return from Englishtown.

Places of Special Interest

1. Englishtown--Site of the noted flea market on weekends. See the Rutgers-Englishtown-Cranbury tour for directions to the flea market and for information about Joe's town sweet shop and soda fountain.

2. Look for the Molly Pitcher well and marker on the right-hand side on the edge of the Monmouth Battleground just before you enter Freehold. This is the well from which Mary Hays or Heis carried water to the soldiers in the decisive battle of Monmouth in 1778. For her heroism, she was nicknamed Molly Pitcher.

3. Allair State Park is on Atlantic Avenue north of where you are entering from Hospital Road. It has picnic and camping facilities.

4. Turkey Swamp park entrance is off Georgia Road--a good place to picnic.

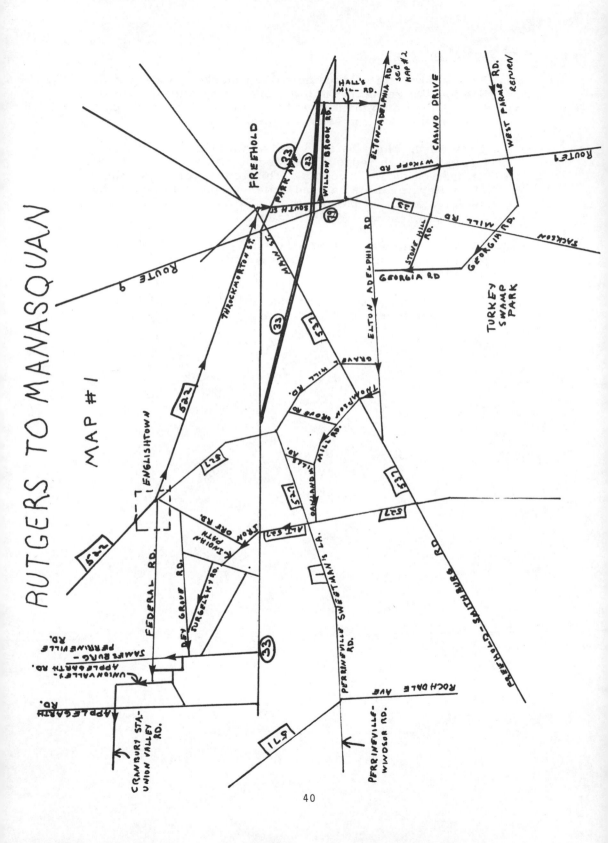

RUTGERS TO MANASQUAN

MAP #1

40

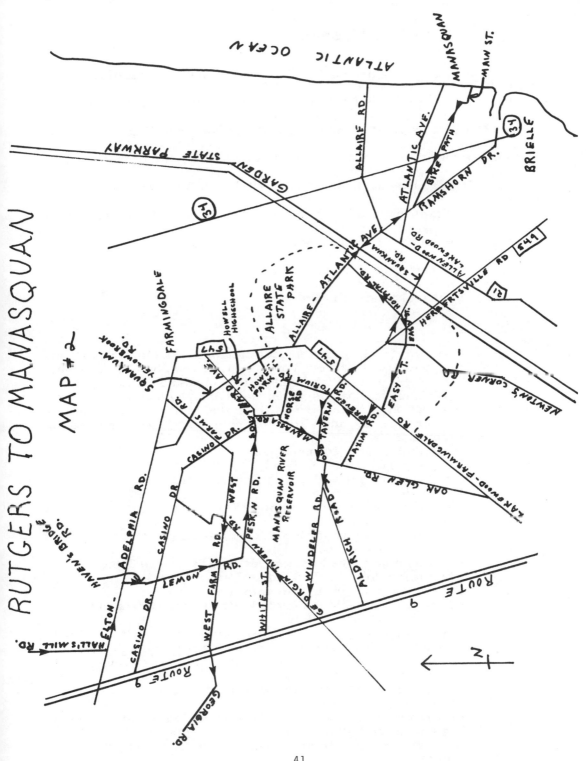

RUTGERS TO MANASQUAN

MAP #2

Tour 7: In and Around Englishtown

The area around Englishtown possesses beautiful glens, woods, and cultivated fields and is well worth a brief tour of its own Cyclists from either Rutgers or Princeton travelling to Englishtown may wish to start early enough to add this tour to their itinerary. People planning to drive to Englishtown for a weekend visit to the flea market may wish to bring along their bikes to explore more than the treasures of the bazaar.

Maximum round-trip distance: 20 miles
Course: mostly flat
Mainimum travel time: 2 hours

Directions:

Begin in front of Joe's soda fountain on Main Street and proceed south through the town (to the right of the store)

Bear right onto Highbridge Road opposite Park Avenue-- Highbridge Road is unmarked here and looks like a continuation of Main Street. It is the right fork immediately after crossing the little concrete bridge over the skating pond.

Right onto Mount Vernon Road

Left onto Tracy Station Road

Continue straight ahead onto Federal Road

Left onto Perrineville Road

Left onto Dey Grove Road (sign is very faded; it is the first road on your left)

Bear right onto unmarked Jurgelsky Road (the first right off Dey Grove Road)

Right onto unmarked Bergen Mills-Gravel Hill Road

First left onto unmarked Indian Path

Cross Dugan's Grove Road onto Iron Ore Road

Cross Route 33 onto the continuation of Iron Ore Road which is called Woodville Road

Cross the intersection of Woodville Road (alt. 527) with county Routes 527 and 1 and take the immediate left onto Oakland Mills Road and follow it as it curves around to the left, avoiding Mill Road

Right at the stop sign onto Sweetman's Lane

Cross Route 33 again

Left at the intersection onto Woodward Road (there is a single sign for Millhurst)

Right onto McCaffery Road (signs were reversed when I was here)

Right onto Iron Ore Road

Bear left onto Highbridge Road into Englishtown.

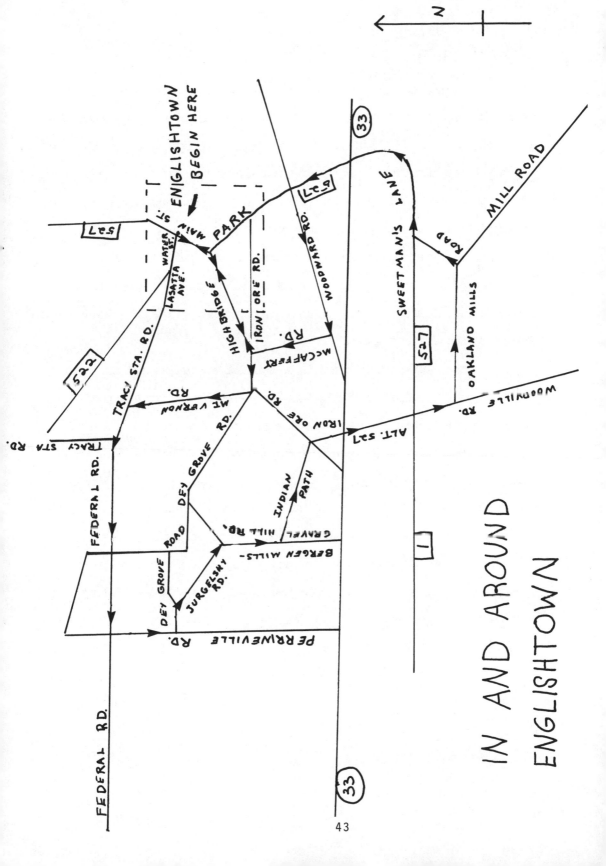

IN AND AROUND
ENGLISHTOWN

PART II: PRINCETON AND SURROUNDINGS

Princeton is the quintessential college town--so beautiful that it might have been thought up by a Hollywood designer as the perfect set for a film about college life. In addition to the fine architecture and lovely campus of the university, the town has a fine collection of historic colonial buildings, good restaurants, and exclusive shops. Above all, the strict zoning laws have prevented the jumble of architectural styles and commercial signs and advertisements characteristic of so many American towns. Without being monotonous, Princeton has a uniformity that gives it charm for resident and visitor alike.

The surrounding area is a cyclist's dream--flat lands and rolling hills, fields and woods--literally a course for everyone. No tour from Princeton is excessively strenuous, but the terrain to the north is more difficult than that to the south. Families with young children or beginning cylists may therefore wish to try the southern tours first--to Cranbury, Englishtown, and Millstone south. The Washington Crossing and Lambertville--New Hope trip takes the cyclist to the beautiful Delaware River and through the rolling hills of southern Hunterdon County. The course to Rocky Hill is along the dream-like Griggstown canal. In short, Princeton offers some of the best opportunities for all around cycling.

Tour 8: Princeton-Rocky Hill Griggstown Canal

A tour north and east of Princeton leading through corn fields, woods, hills, and rich suburban settlements. It ends with a ride along the historic Griggstown Canal. There are a few hills of moderate difficulty as distinguished from the Cranbury tour, which is virtually flat. A variation of this tour is given in the Rutgers-Princeton section-the return to Rutgers being via Great Road.

Maximum round trip distance: 35 miles
Course: rolling hills, a few fairly steep
Minimum travel time: 4 hours

Directions:

> Begin at the main gate of Princeton University in front of Nassau Hall,
> Go left on Nassau Street (Route 27 south)
> Bear left onto Stockton Street in the direction of Lawrence-ville-Trenton
> Right onto Elm Road in the direction of Hopewell (Elm Road becomes Great Road, which now has a bicycle path separated from the main road by a concrete barrier)
> Left onto North Road
> Left onto Pretty Brook Road (up hill here)
> Left onto Province Line Road and immediate right onto continuation of Pretty Brook Road, which becomes Cleveland Road
> Right at the stop sign onto Hopewell Road (County Route 569)
> At the fork--bear left onto Crusher Road
> Cross Route 518 spur diagonally to the right onto Van Dyck Road (up hill here)
> Cross the Lambertville-Hopewell Road (County Route 518) onto the continuation of Van Dyck Road
> Right onto Featherbed Lane
> Left onto the Hopewell-Wertsville Road (County Route 607)
> Right onto Ridge Road
> Right onto Lindbergh Road (signs are reversed here) (up hill)
> Left onto Zion Road
> Right onto Hollow Road

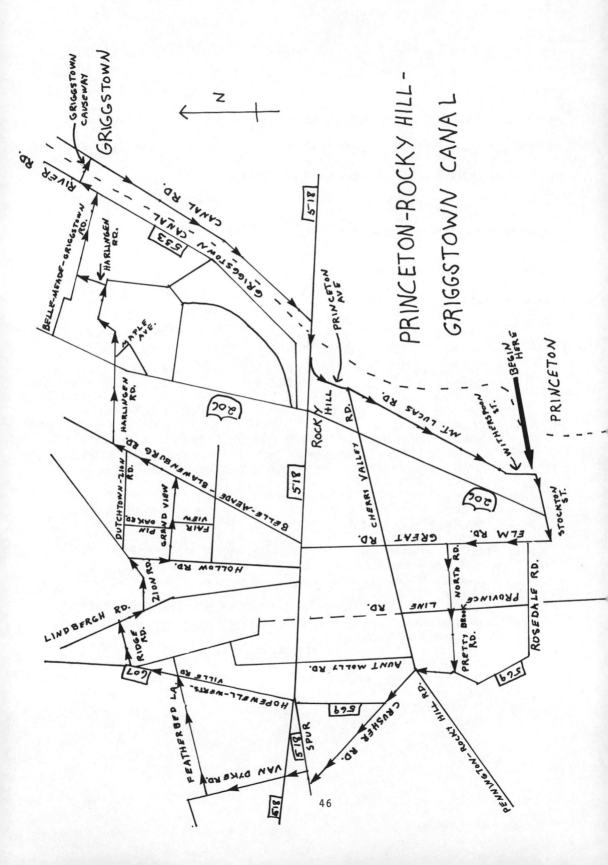

PRINCETON–ROCKY HILL – GRIGGSTOWN CANAL

Left onto Grand View Road at the little white steel bridge*
Left onto BelleMeade-Blawenburg Road
Right onto Dutchtown-Harlingen Road
Cross Route 206 onto the continuation of Harlingen Road
Bear left at the Maple Street fork to continue on course on
  Harlingen Road (Harlingen Road has a brief patch of
  gravel lasting 2/10 of a mile)
Left onto the continuation of Harlingen Road at the intersec-
  tion of Harlingen and Mill Pond Roads
Right onto the BelleMeade-Griggstown Road
Left onto River Road
Right (almost immediately) onto the iron bridge of the
  Griggstown Causeway
Right at the Griggstown General Store onto Canal Road (the
  general store has excellent sandwiches and you may also
  rent a canoe for a trip on the canal)
Right onto Route 518 (Washington Street of Rocky Hill)
Left onto Princeton Avenue at the Rocky Hill Inn
Bear left at the fork onto Mt. Lucas Road
Follow into Witherspoon Street and back to Nassau Street
  in Princeton

---

*Alternative: You may continue on Grand View down the hill or you
  may go left up the hill onto Pin Oak Road and then
  right onto the Dutchtown-Zion Road, a long, steep
  descent which has a more remote and rural feeling
  than Grand View. At the end of Zion Road, left onto
  the Belle Meade-Blawenburg Road and immediate
  right onto the Dutchtown-Harlingen Road. Follow remaining directions above.

Tour 9: Princeton-Washington Crossing-New Hope
with an Alternative Return from Lambertville to
Hopewell and a Short Princeton-Pennington Tour

Beginning in Princeton, this tour takes you through rolling hills and green countryside to the site of Washington's famous crossing of the Delaware River in 1776. After a stop in Washington Crossing State Park, you yourself cross the Delaware on the narrow iron bridge to Pennsylvania and ride up the river bank to New Hope-Lambertville, a concentration of boutiques, restaurants, art galleries and the site of the Bucks County Playhouse. You then recross the Delaware at Stockton and ride back to Princeton through the beautiful, rolling countryside of lower Hunterdon County. If you make a overnight trip of it, you will want to consult the tour-"Lambertville-New Hope and Surrounding Area."

Maximum round-trip distance: 60 miles
Course: Rolling hills with a few steep ones
Minimum travel time: 7 hours

Directions:

> From the main gate of Princeton University in front of Nassau Hall, take Nassau Street (Route 27) south
> Bear left onto Stockton Street (1) in the direction of Lawrenceville-Trenton (Route 206 south)
> Right onto Elm Road in the direction of Hopewell
> Left onto Rosedale Road
> Left at the stop sign onto Carter Road in the direction of Lawrenceville
> Right onto Cold Soil Road
> Right onto Blackwell Road
> Right onto Federal City road
> At the "yield" sign, continue straight ahead onto East Delaware Avenue in Pennington
> Cross Route 31 and continue straight ahead onto the Pennington-Titusville Road
> Left at the stop sign onto unmarked Bear tavern Road (County Road 579)

Right at the stop light in the direction of the entrance to the park.

Right into the park (2)

Left in the direction of the Visitors Center and Flag Museum. At the Flag Museum continue around to the left and uphill to the overlook

Cross the lawn to the pedestrian bridge over Route 29

Cross the Delaware via the iron bridge-walk your bike

Right onto River Road (Highway 32) north in the direction of New Hope

In New Hope (3) continue on Route 32 north

Bear right where Route 32 goes left to recross the Delaware into Stockton, New Jersey

Left onto the Main Street of Stockton (County Route 29 north)

Right at the sign "Seargentsville-Flemington" onto County Route 523 (uphill here)

(If you desire to see the last remaining public covered bridge in New Jersey--included in the Lambertville-New Hope section--take your second left onto unmarked Covered Bridge Road, which intersects County Route 604, which runs through the covered bridge. After inspecting the bridge, take 604--a right turn from Covered Bridge Road--into Seargentsville and follow instructions below from there.)

In Seargentsville, right onto Route 604 in direction of Ringoes

Right onto John Ringoe Road (County Route 579)

In Ringoes, watch for Mom's Restaurant on your left at the intersection of County Routes 579, 179, and 31

Left just beyond the restaurant onto Wertsville Road (County Route 602)

Cross Routes 202 and 31 to remain on County Route 602

Right at the sign to Hopewell (County Route 607)

Left at the traffic light in Hopewell onto West Broad Street

Continue through Hopewell striaght onto County Route 518

Right onto Cherry Hill Road

Left onto Cherry Valley Road and immediately right onto the continuation of Cherry Hill Road

Cross Route 206 at the light and turn right onto Mt. Lucas Road, which becomes Witherspoon Street leading into Nassau Street, Princeton

Alternative return to Hopewell-Princeton from Lambertville

Instead of going up the Delaware on the Pennsylvania side, cross the bridge to Lambertville.

Right onto New Jersey 29 South in direction of Washington Crossing and Trenton

49

Left onto Quarry Street, which is the Lambertville-Rocktown Road (this at the sign saying Hopewell, but avoid
County Route 518, instead take Quarry Street, which runs
parallel to the left of 518)

Cross the Mt. Airy-Harbortown Road by the South Hunterdon Regional High School

Cross County Route 31 onto the Rocktown Road

At the fork, bear right onto Mountain Road (unmarked)

Left onto Linvale Road

Right onto Orchard Road (a few patches of gravel)

Bear left onto Runyan Mill Road

Right at the stop sign onto Saddle Shop Road

Right at the intersection onto County Route 607, which leads
into Hopewell-- a trip of approximately 14 miles, only
about 2 miles longer than the more direct, but heavily
travelled 518-- well worth the extra distance.

Princeton-Pennington-Hopewell: A Short Tour

For those who do not wish to go all the way to New Hope,

but want to enjoy part of the area to the west of Princeton the

following is an alternative:

Follow the Princeton-Washington Crossing-New Hope directions to the Pennington-Titusville Road, which begins
just after crossing Route 31. Follow the Pennington-
Titusville Road briefly and turn-

Right onto Scotch Road which becomes Burd Road beyond
the intersection

Left onto Woosamonsa Road

Right onto Poor Farm Road (uphill here)

Right onto unmarked Woodsville Road

Left onto New Road

Right onto Route 518 and follow to Hopewell

Follow instructions in the main Washington Crossing-New
Hope Tour for return to Princeton.

Places of Special Interest

1. Site of Morven, the residence of the governor of New
Jersey. Built in 1701, the house was the residence of
Richard Stockton, one of the signers of the Declaration
of Independence.

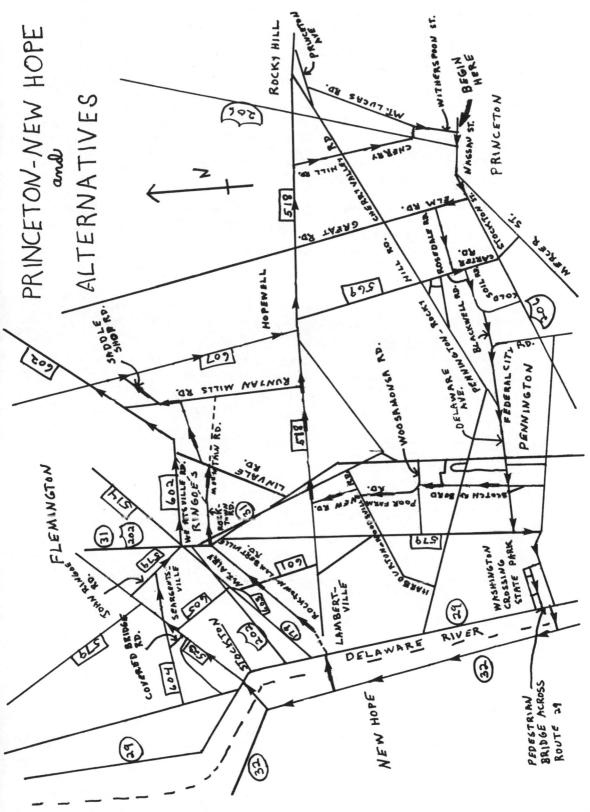

PRINCETON-NEW HOPE and ALTERNATIVES

2. Washington Crossing State Park with its picnic groves, nature center and open-air theater, the park is well worth touring. The Visitor Center has an electrified map with a slide display and sound narrative explaining the events surrounding the crossing of the Delaware. The Flag Museum shows the evolution of the United States flag. You may also visit Ferry House, which was the home of the ferry keeper and also served as a tavern. It was here that Washington and his staff planned the attack on Trenton while their 2400 men crossed the Delaware.

3. New Hope and Lambertville-- a collection of boutiques, ice cream parlors, antique shops and fine restaurants catering to vacationers and residents of Bucks County, Pennsylvania. It is also the site of the Bucks County Playhouse, one of the best theaters in the summer straw-hat circuit.

Tour 10: Princeton to Englishtown

From Princeton, the tourer pedals to Kingston and then alongside beautiful Lake Carnegie. The corn and grain fields surrounding Cranbury add to the rustic pleasure of this "rural ride." There is some necessary duplication of the Rutgers-Englishtown tour, but the trip from Princeton is different enough that enthusiastic cyclists may want to make both. And, as in the former case, Princeton cyclists may wish to combine this tour with the "In and Around Englishtown" trip, so start early.

Maximum roundtrip distance: 50 miles
Course: mostly flat
Minimum travel time: 6 hours

Directions:

As with all tours beginning in Princeton, this one also starts at the university gate in front of Nassau Hall. Facing away from the gate, go right on Nassau Street north in the direction of Kingston. In Kingston, just before you reach the crest of the hill--

Right onto Academy Street (opposite the Kingston post office)

Cross Route 1 in the direction of Plainsboro

Continue through Plainsboro (1) onto the Plainsboro Road

In Cranbury, continue straight ahead across Main Street

Left onto Maplewood Avenue and

Immediate right in the direction of Jamesburg and Camden

Cross Route 130 onto the Cranbury-Half Acre Road

Cross Applegarth Road

Bear left to remain on Half Acre Road at the junction with Union Valley-Half Acre Road

Right at the stop sign onto unmarked Prospect Plains Road (you will see a sign for the Perrineville Road)

Right onto Perrineville Road

Left onto unmarked Gravel Hill Road (the continuation of Union Valley Road), which is the first left off of the Perrineville Road

Bear right at the intersection in the direction of Englishtown

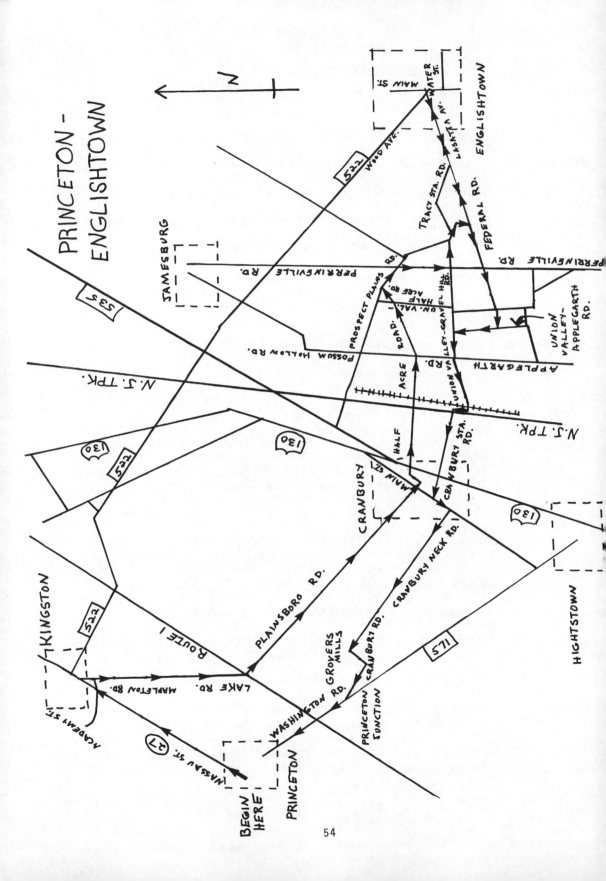

PRINCETON – ENGLISHTOWN

54

Left at the stop sign onto unmarked Federal Road and follow into Englishtown (2) (Federal Road becomes La Satta Avenue which merges with Water Street in Englishtown)

To return to Princeton:

Return to Water Street and retrace your route, bearing left onto La Satta Avenue

Continue straight ahead onto Federal Road

Right onto Union Valley-Applegarth Road when Federal Road ends

Left onto Union Valley Road in the direction of Cranbury

Continue straight ahead at the intersection onto Cranbury Station Road

Right at the railroad crossing over the railroad tracks (if you see a faded street sign saying Halsey Reed Road, you have gone too far, go back and cross the railroad tracks)

Right at the stop sign just after the crossing and follow the road around across the New Jersey Turnpike (you should see the large Firestone plant in front of you)

Cross Route 130 and continue straight ahead into Cranbury

Left onto Main Street

Right onto Cranbury Neck Road which becomes Cranbury Road in Grover's Mill

Right at the traffic light onto the Heightstown Road (County Route 571) in the direction of Princeton

Cross Route 1 at the circle and continue onto Washington Road and into Princeton

Places of Special Interest

1. Note the Lapidus Market in Plainsboro, which makes excellent sandwiches.

2. Englishtown is the site of the noted weekend flea market, which can be reached by going left onto Main Street and bearing left at the Exxon station.

Tour 11: Princeton-Millstone South

A tour through the beautiful fields and woods south of Princeton. The route takes the cyclist through the Mercer County Central Park to the Assunpink Wildlife Management Area, a place remote and isolated in feeling. The return is via the beautiful Perrineville Road, which runs through an area virtually untouched by suburban developers. No doubt the bulldozers are impatiently racing their engines so enjoy it while you can. As with most of the southerly routes, the terrain is gentle and good for families and younger riders.

Maximum round-trip distance: 35 miles
Course: mostly flat
Minimum travel time: 4 hours

Directions:

> Begin at the main gate of Princeton University in front of Nassau Hall
> Right onto Nassau Street (County Route 27 north in the direction of Kingston)
> Right onto Washington Road (opposite the Garden Cinema), which runs next to the Firestone Library in the direction of Princeton Junction
> Cross Route 1 at the traffic circle onto the continuation of Washington Road which is now called the Hightstown Road (County Routes 526/571)
> Bear left at the fork in the direction of Hightstown-Freehold
> Right onto unmarked Clarksville Road (the sign is across the street) which is the first right after Alexander Road (you will see the West Windsor-Plainsboro High School on your left).
Left onto the North Post road
Cross Village Road
Left onto Conover Road
Right onto the Edinburg Road
Right onto the Old Trenton Road
Immediate left onto the Robinsville Road

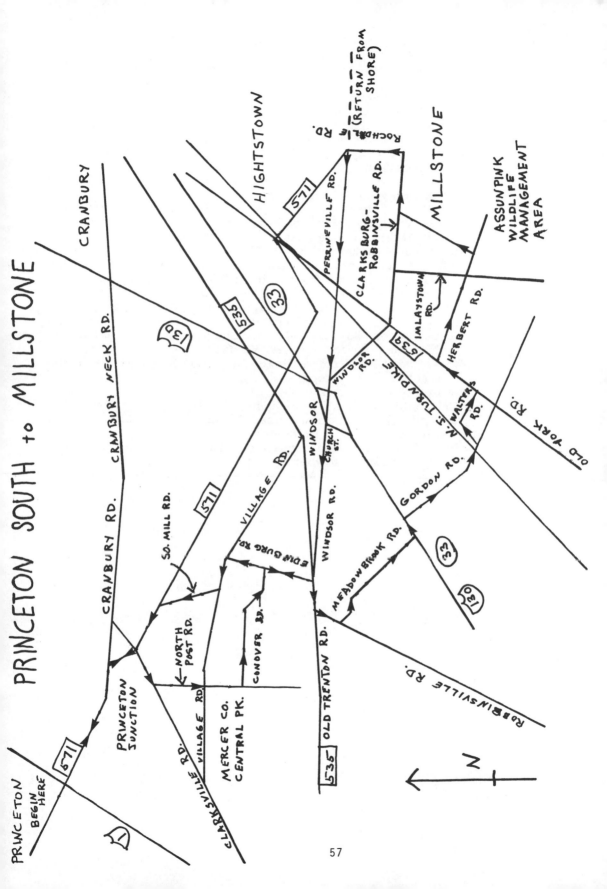

PRINCETON SOUTH to MILLSTONE

Left onto Meadowbrook Road (light gravel here for one mile)

Left onto County Route 130

Immediate right onto Gordon Road

Immediately after crossing the overpass over the New Jersey Turnpike, left onto unmarked Walter's Road

Left onto County Route 539 (Old York Road) at the end of Walters Road

First right onto unmarked Herbert Road

Cross Imlaystown Road

Bear left at the fork where you see the sign for the Assunpink Wildlife Management Area (road becomes hard packed dirt for one mile)

Right onto Clarksburg Road

Left onto unmarked Rochdale Avenue (simply follow the pavement to the left as road in front of you becomes dirt)

Left onto the Perrineville Road and cross all intersections--including the New Jersey Turnpike--to its end

At the end of Perreniville Road, right onto Windsor Road

Cross Routes 33 and 130 onto Church Street in Windsor, which once again becomes Windsor Road

Cross the Old Trenton Road onto Edinburg Road in the direction of Princeton

Left onto Village Road

Right onto South Mill Road in the direction of Princeton

Left onto the Hightstown Road (County routes 526 and 571) in the direction of Princeton

Cross Route 1 at the circle onto Washington Road and return to Princeton where you began.

Tour 12: Princeton-Cranbury: A Roundabout Way

Another "southern" tour through cultivated fields and farms. Although the destination is the town of Cranbury, the route is anything but direct. Rather it is a zigzag course through the fields--a leisurely ride for people seeking something that is not too strenuous. Mostly flat, families with small children who ride will find this a good course. However, I have encountered racers speeding along these back roads, their flatness allowing them to attain sustained high speeds.

Maximum round-trip distance: 35 miles
Course: mostly flat
Minimum travel time: 4 hours

Directions:

> From the main gate of Princeton University in front of
> Nassau Hall, left onto Nassau Street in the direction of
> Kingston (Route 27 north)
> In Kingston, right at the traffic light onto Heathcoat Road in
> the direction of Monmouth Junction
> Cross Route 1 in the direction of Monmouth Junction onto
> Route 522 which becomes Ridge Road
> Continue through the center of Monmouth Junction past the
> IBM plant and at the stop sign, make a "U" turn to the
> right onto Culver Road
> Left onto Friendship Road (when Culver Road ends)
> Right onto Miller road
> Right onto Broadway (unmarked) at the end of Miller Road
> First left onto Eiker road (unmarked)
> Right onto Dey Road (unmarked) at the end of Eiker road
> Left (at the stop sign) onto the Plainsboro Road
> Right onto Main Street in Cranbury
> Pass through the town
> Right onto Cranbury Neck Road, which becomes Cranbury
> Road in Grover's Mill
> Right at the stop light in the direction of Princeton onto
> the Hightstown Road, which become Washington Road into
> Princeton (County Route 521)*

---

*Alternatives to cut trip short by about ten miles:
> Instead of turning right, go left onto Dey Road, immediate
> right onto Petty Road,
> left onto the Plainsboro Road into Cranbury

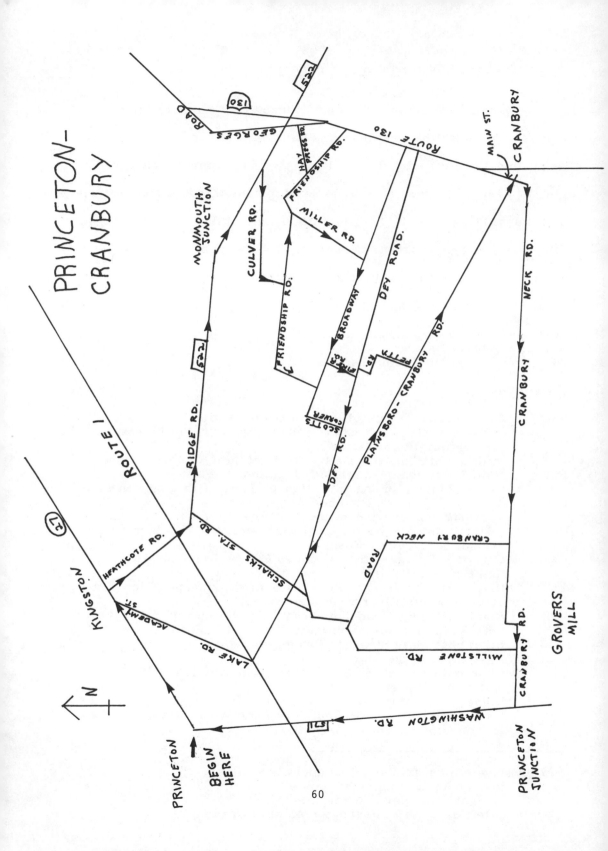

PRINCETON-
CRANBURY

Tour 13: Princeton to the Shore at Manasquan

A tour on back roads through wooded areas and beautiful fields to one of the beaches closest to Princeton. As is typical of much of the Jersey shore, Manasquan has a lovely beach, but it is also lined with concessions, hot dog stands, and "amusements." If you want a quieter scene, bike the sixteen miles down the shore to Island Beach State Park, which is as beautiful as Cape Cod or Fire Island.

If you would like a short trip of a few days duration, you might consider biking to Rutgers-New Brunswick (see the Rutgers-Princeton tour). Follow directions to Sandy Hook in the Rutgers-to-Sandy Hook tour and then bike down the coast to Manasquan and home to Princeton.

The present tour has some necessary overlapping with the Rutgers-Mannasquan trip, but there are some alternate routes given there that you might wish to consider. The return to Princeton is through the beautiful area around the Mercer County Park and the Assunpink Wildlife Management Area.

Maximum round-trip distance: 90 miles
Course; mostly flat
Minimum travel time: 10 hours

Directions:

> The trip to Manasquan is via Englishtown. See the Prince-ton-Englishtown tour for directions to Englishtown, the first leg of the shore tour. In Englishtown from Water Street
> Right onto Main Street

61

Left at the stop light onto Tennent Avenue in the direction of Freehold. Tennent Avenue becomes the Freehold Road (1) which in turn becomes Throckmorton Street in Freehold

Cross Broad Street, the railroad tracks, and West Main Street

Right onto South Street

Go under the big Route 33 overpass and take your

Immediate left onto Willowbrook Road (if you find yourself suddenly on busy Route 9, you have gone too far)

Right onto Hall's Mill Road

Left onto the Elton Adelphia Road (see map #2)

Right onto Haven Bridge Road

Bear left onto Casino Drive

Cross West Farms Road to continue on Casino Drive

Left onto Peskin Road, which becomes Southard Avenue

Right at the Howell Regional High School onto the Squankum-Yellowbrook Road

Right at the intersection onto County Routes 524/547

Immediately left in the direction of G.L. Thompson Medical Home (unmarked Allaire Road-Atlantic Avenue, which is the continuation of County Route 524) (2)

At the intersection where Atlantic Avenue bears left, continue straight ahead onto Ramshorn Drive.*

Here you will see the beginning of the bikeway on your left leading to Manasquan

At the end of the bikeway--

Right onto the street and follow it around to the left onto Main Street

Follow Main Street to the beach.

To return to Princeton:

Return to the bikeway via Main Street at the end of the bikeway, go north on Atlantic Avenue

Left onto Hospital Road

Cross County Route 21 onto unmarked Easy Street--the continuation of Hospital Road

Cross two more intersections and follow Easy Street to its end

Right onto County Route 547--the Lakewood-Farmingdale Road

Left onto the Oak Glen-Maxim Road

Right onto Preventorium Road

Left onto Old Tavern Road

Right onto Aldrich Road

At the fork, bear right (really straight ahead) onto unmarked Windeler Road

Right onto Georgia Tavern Road just past the Land O'Pines School

Left onto Lemon Road

Left onto West Farms Road (see map #1)

Cross Route 9 onto the continuation of West Farms Road, which becomes Georgia Road (3)

Cross busy Jackson Mill Road

Left onto the Elton-Adelphia Road (County Route 524)

Right onto Thompson's Grove Road

Cross Route 537 onto the continuation of Thompson's Grove Road

Bear left onto Mill Road at the fork

Left onto Oakland Mills Road

Right at the end of Oakland Mills Road

Immediate left onto County Route 1 which is Sweetman's Lane-a lovely rural route-which eventually becomes the Perrineville Road

At the intersection with Rochdale Avenue (County Route 571) where the main road curves to the right, continue straight ahead onto the continuation of Perrineville Road, which becomes the Perrineville-Windsor Road. Continue on the Perrineville Road across all intersections (you will over-pass the New Jersey Turnpike) until its end

(See the "Princeton South to Millstone" map for this section of the return to Princeton)

Right onto Windsor Road

Cross Routes 130/33 into the town of Windsor (Church Street) and continue straight ahead

At the traffic light, cross Old Trenton Road onto Edinburg Road in the direction of Princeton

Left onto Village Road

Right onto South Mill Road in the direction of Princeton

Left onto County Routes 526/571 in the direction of Princeton

Cross Route 1 at the Circle onto Washington Road and return to your starting point in Princeton.

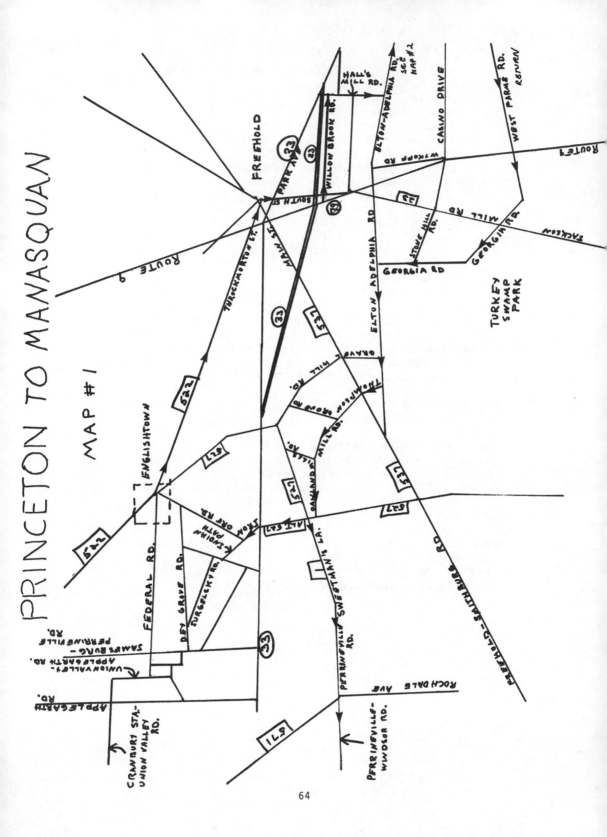

PRINCETON TO MANASQUAN

MAP #1

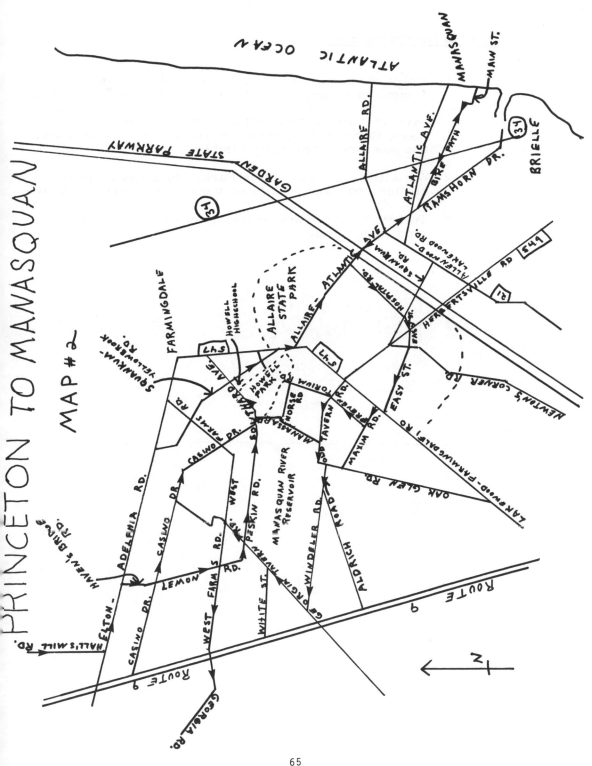

PRINCETON TO MANASQUAN

MAP #2

65

Places of Special Interest

1. Molly Pitcher Well on the Freehold Road next to the Monmouth battlefield on the right-hand side just before you enter Freehold. This is the well from which Mary Hays or Heis carried water to the soldiers in the decisive Battle of Monmouth in 1778. For her heroism, she was nicknamed Molly Pitcher.

2. You will pass Allaire State Park, which has camping facilities and was the site of the historic Howell Works

3. Turkey Swamp Park entrance is on Georgia Road, a good place to picnic.

PART III: THE HILLS OF HUNTERDON COUNTY

Although it is being rapidly "developed," Hunterdon County abounds with farms, horse ranches, and old colonial homesteads. Its hills are sometimes taxing, but not as strenuous as the genuine mountains of Warren and Sussex counties to the north. The cyclist who is in moderately good shape should have little trouble, but it is an area to be avoided by the once-a-month rider. Beautiful vistas, green meadows, rushing brooks, and narrow country lanes make this one of the most beautiful areas accessible to the average cyclist. The Spruce Run and Round Valley recreation areas offer swimming, camping, and boating. Many will want to return again and may desire to work out alternate routes with the aid of the maps.

Tour 14: Whitehouse Station-Round Valley Reservoir

Two challenging hills, magnificent vistas, small country lanes, and villages nestled in hills abounding with brooks and streams make this a truly spectacular and varied tour. Both professional tourers and families on an outing will find this a worthwhile and rewarding trip. There is even a sandy beach with food services and excellent facilities for changing and showering. Be sure and bring a swimsuit for a mid-ride swim, especially since entrance is free to cyclists. Whitehouse Station may be reached via U.S. Route 22 and is about 45 miles from New York City. You may park your car near the train station or in the lot near the V.F.W. Post.

Maximum round-trip distance: 35 miles
Course: rolling, sometimes hilly; two steep hills
Minimum travel time: 4 hours

Directions:

> Leave Whitehouse Station south on Main Street-County Route
>   523 (away from Route 22)
> Right onto Dreahook Road
> Left onto Lebanon Road where Dreahook Road ends
> Right onto County Route 629 (at the intersection is a country
>   store) (1)
> Route 629 passes by Round Valley Area (2)
> Left on Route 22
> Right onto unmarked Petticoat Lane at large sign saying
>   "Youth Correctional Institution-Annandale."
> At stop sign, stay on course in direction of Cokesbury
> Bear right at intersection and enter the village of Cokesbury
> Left onto Water Street (3) in the direction of Mountainville

Alternative routes:

> From Mountainville, you may shorten or lengthen your trip
>   as desired by following one of several alternative routes.
>   You may save a minimum of 9 miles by going right.

68

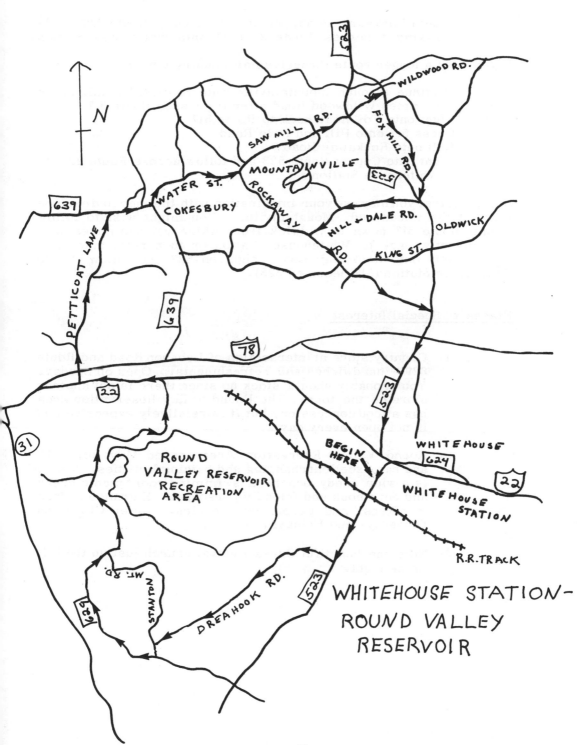

N

523

WILDWOOD RD.

FOX HILL RD.

523

SAW MILL RD.

WATER ST.
COKESBURY

MOUNTAINVILLE

ROCKAWAY

639

MILL & DALE RD.

OLDWICK

RD.

KING ST.

639

PETTICOAT LANE

78

523

22

31

ROUND
VALLEY RESERVOIR
RECREATION
AREA

BEGIN
HERE

WHITEHOUSE

624

22

WHITEHOUSE
STATION

R.R. TRACK

629

STANTON

MT. RD.

DREAHOOK RD.

523

WHITEHOUSE STATION-
ROUND VALLEY
RESERVOIR

onto Rockaway Road, right onto County Route 523, following it across Route 22 back into Whitehouse Station

If you wish a longer route through small country lanes:

> Continue through Mountainville onto Saw Mill Road, which becomes Wildwood Road after it crosses Route 517
> Right onto Fox Road back to Route 517
> Cross 517 onto Hill and Dale Road
> Left onto Rockaway Road
> Right onto County Route 523 and follow across Route 22 into Whitehouse Station

If you desire, you may use your imagination with the map and explore more of the woods and Mountainville. You might wish to follow County Route 517 down to Oldwick from which you can either proceed directly back to Whitehouse Station or turn right onto King Street, left onto Rockaway Road, right on 523 and follow it into Whitehouse Station (517 becomes 523).

Places of Special Interest

1. Country store at intersection of Lebanon Road and Route 629-- sandwiches and refreshments. Open on Sunday. You probably should stock up since there is not another store on the tour. The Round Valley Reservation area has a food concession, but it is relatively expensive and is not open every day.

2. Round Valley Recreation Area opened May 30, 1977 and has excellent changing and bathing facilities. There is a wide sandy beach, a swimming pool, picnic areas and courteous and friendly personnel. Entrance is free to hikers and people on bicycles. Note: Closed on Thursdays and Fridays.

3. Note the beautiful Greek Revival church just up the hill to the right.

Tour 15:   Spruce Run-Lockwood Gorge

A tour around another of the reservoirs of Hunterdon County. While not as spectacular as the Round Valley reservoir tour, this trip runs through the Lockwood Gorge, the site of the beautiful, remote South Branch of the Raritan River. The road that runs alongside it is rather rough and rocky, but the scenery is well worth the inconvenience. The tour begins in the town of Clinton and is typical of Hunterdon County--rolling hills with a few steep inclines. You may reach Clinton from either U.S. Route 22 or Interstate 78--both of which merge just before the Clinton exit.*

Maximum round-trip distance: 40 miles
Course: rolling hills, some steep
Minimum travel time: 5 hours

Directions:

      Park in the A & P parking lot, which will be found shortly
        after exiting from I-78 and is located on Old Route 22
      Right onto Old Route 22
      Right onto Halstead Street
      Cross Main Street
      Right onto Center Street
      Left onto Gray Rock Road (immediately before the sign for
        New Jersey Route 31 to Trenton and Annandale) Gray
        Rock Road is disected (literally cut in two) by Interstate
        78 and Route 31. To reach the continuation of Gray Rock
        Road, you must turn right onto I-78 for only a few yards
        and take the Annandale exit which will take you across
        78 and then left onto 31 north in the direction of
        Washington. Then take the immediate right onto the con-
        continuation of Gray Rock Road.
      Right onto Old Jericho Road (about 100 feet of gravel here)
      Left at the "yield" sign; cross the stream and turn

---

*If you want to swim in the reservoir recreation areas, you must use Spruce Run on Thursday and Friday since Round Valley is closed on those days.

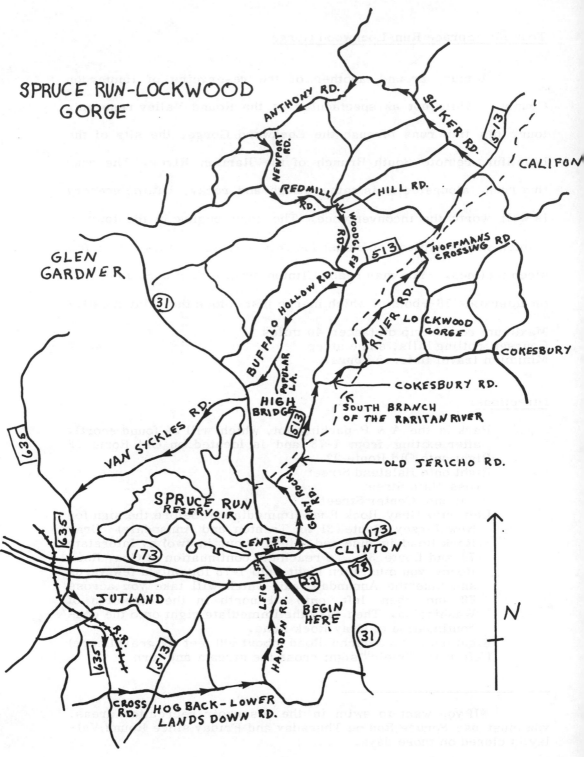

SPRUCE RUN-LOCKWOOD
GORGE

ANTHONY RD.

SLIKER RD.

S-13

CALIFON

NEWPORT RD.

REDMILL RD.

HILL RD.

WOODGLEN RD.

513

HOFFMANS CROSSING RD.

GLEN GARDNER

31

BUFFALO HOLLOW RD.

RIVER RD.

LOCKWOOD GORGE

COKESBURY

COKESBURY RD.

POPULAR LA.

HIGH BRIDGE

513

SOUTH BRANCH OF THE RARITAN RIVER

639

VAN SYCKLES RD.

OLD JERICHO RD.

GRAD ROCK RD.

SPRUCE RUN RESERVOIR

635

173

CENTER ST.

CLINTON

173

78

33

JUTLAND

R.R.

635

513

LEIGH ST.

HAMDEN RD.

BEGIN HERE

31

N

CROSS RD.

HOG BACK-LOWER LANDS DOWN RD.

Right onto County Route 513, which is West Main Street of High Bridge

Right onto Cokesbury Road and into the Lockwood Gorge. The road through the gorge is hardpacked dirt for two miles, but the beauty of the gorge is worth the inconvenience.

Left onto Hoffmans Crossing Road (over the bridge and up the hill)

Right onto County Route 513

Left onto Sliker Road in Califon

Bear left onto Anthony Road

Left onto Newport Road

Pass Dewey Lane and bear left to continue on course on Newport Road

Left onto Red Mill Road

Left onto Hill Road

Right onto Woodglen Road and pass the Woodglen School

Right onto County Route 513--proceed for about 100 feet and

Right onto Buffalo Hollow Road (sign very faint and old)

Bear right at intersection of Popular Lane to remain on course on Buffalo Hallow Road (signs were reversed when I was there), which here suddenly opens up to a beautiful vista of the valley and Spruce Run Reservoir.

Left onto Route 31 and follow signs to Spruce Run

Right onto Van Syckles Road (some traffic on weekends because of recreation area)

Left at the stop sign beside sign saying "To New Jersey 78" onto County Road 635

Cross Routes 173, 22 and 78

Right at sign for Jutland to stay on course

Bear left at the fork in the direction of Jutland

Left immediately after crossing railroad track to stay on course

Left onto Cook's Cross Road, which becomes Hogback Road after you cross Route 513 and then becomes Lower Landsdown Road after you cross Route 617.

Left at end of Lower Landsdown Road onto Hamden Road in the direction of Clinton

Right onto Old Route 22 in order to return to the A & P parking lot.

Tour 16: Flemington to Lambertville-New Hope

A tour through the beautiful southwestern area of Hunterdon County. Less strenuous than the hilly northern regions, there are nevertheless enough steep hills for a challenging ride, especially at the beginning. If you decide to make an overnight tour of it, you can camp in the Bull's Island State Recreation Area near Stockton. If you are well-heeled, you can stay in the lovely 1740 House in Lumberville, Pennsylvania north of New Hope on Route 32. The Black Bass Hotel next door is an excellent place to eat, but costly. If you decide to economize by camping in Bull's Island, but want to splurge on a fine meal, you can cross the Delaware River on the beautiful pedestrian bridge directly to the Black Bass Hotel and restaurant. If you decide to remain in the area, you should consult the trip in this book entitled "In and Around Lambertville-New Hope," which includes Seargentsville and the last remaining public covered bridge in New Jersey. To reach Flemington by car, take U.S. Route 202 to the Flemington exit. Park in any one of a number of super market parking lots.

Maximum round-trip distance: 55 miles
Course: rolling hills; a few steep grades
Minimum travel time: 7 hours

> The tour begins in front of the Hunterdon County Courthouse in Flemington. Facing away from the courthouse, go to your left on Main Street past the post office.
> Bear left at the fork where the Gettysburg Monument and Presbyterian Church stand onto North Main Street
> Continue on North Main Street up the long, difficult hill out of Flemington- your reward is the fine view of the valley below

North Main Street becomes County Route 617

Left at the stop sign and intersection onto the continuation of 617 in the direction of Cherryville

Left in Cherryville onto Quakertown Road (County Route 616) with its beautiful views of distant mountains

Pedal through Quaker Town and just as the town ends
Left onto Locust Grove Road

Right when Locust Grove Road ends onto County Route 615 in the direction of Pittstown for about 100 yards

Left onto Baker Road

Left at the end of Baker Road onto unmarked Senator Stout Road

Here you may choose one of two alternatives--you may bear right onto Oak Summit Road and then left onto County Route 519 and follow it directly south to Rosemont and Stockton--or you may take the following country roads which parallel 519, but which have less traffic and are a bit more scenic. It is easy to get lost however--here is the "country road" route:

Where Senator Stout Road bears right onto Oak Summit Road, continue straight ahead onto the little rough connecting road and

Left onto unmarked Hampton Road, which makes a sharp right--follow it as it curves to the left and to the right

Right onto Oak Grove Road

Left onto County Route 519 (Kingwood Road) through Baptistown

Cross Route 12 and Firehouse Lane

Take your first left onto unmarked Union Road

Left onto the Barbertown Road

First right (after only 3/4 mile) onto Hammar Road--a lovely wooded road

Right at the first intersection onto the Locktown-Kingwood Road

Left onto Route 519 and follow into Rosemont and to Stockton

Left onto Route 29 south in Stockton

Right in Stockton onto Bridge Street and cross the Delaware River

Left onto Pennsylvania Route 32 south and proceed Hope

Left in New Hope onto the bridge to recross the Delaware into Lambertville

Left onto Route 29 north

You will soon see the large overpass of Route 202, but just before you would go under 202, turn

Right onto Headquarters Road (this looks like a ramp to 202, but it is not, for it soon becomes the extremely narrow Headquarters Road)

75

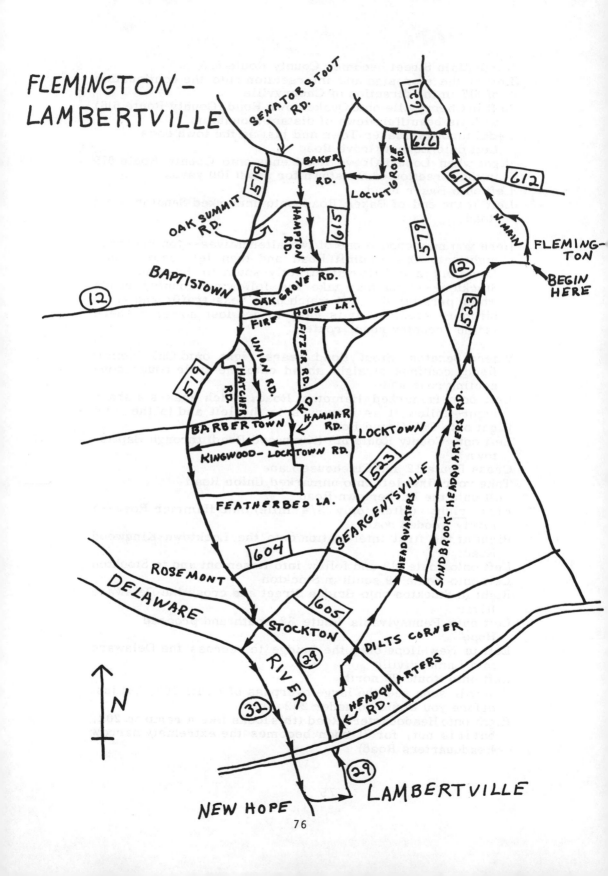

FLEMINGTON –
LAMBERTVILLE

SENATOR STOUT RD.

621

616

617

612

519

BAKER RD.

LOCUST GROVE RD.

615

579

N. MAIN

FLEMING-
TON

OAK SUMMIT RD.

HAMPTON RD.

12

BEGIN
HERE

BAPTISTOWN

OAK GROVE RD.

12

OAK GROVE RD.

HOUSE LA.

523

FIRE

FITZER RD.

519

THATCHER RD.

UNION RD.

RD.

HAMMAR RD.

LOCKTOWN

BARBERTOWN

KINGWOOD – LOCKTOWN RD.

523

SEARGENTSVILLE

HEADQUARTERS

SANDBROOK – HEADQUARTERS RD.

FEATHERBED LA.

604

ROSEMONT

605

DELAWARE

STOCKTON

29

DILTS CORNER

RIVER

32

HEADQUARTERS RD.

29

N

NEW HOPE

LAMBERTVILLE

Right at the first intersection onto the continuation of the
Headquarters Road. (If you go straight ahead, you will
be on Seabrook Road which soon becomes unpaved).
Cross County Route 605 in Dilts Corner and continue
straight ahead)
Right onto County Route 604
Left onto the Sandbrook-Headquarters Road, the first paved
road to the left
Right onto County Route 523 and follow back into Flem-
ington--about 4 miles.

Tour 17: Lambertville-New Hope and Surrounding Area

This tour assumes that you are spending a day or so in the Lambertville-New Hope area and wish to explore its countryside. Or you may drive directly to Lambertville-New Hope. I suggest you park on the Lambertville side since it is less congested than New Hope. This course takes you along the beautiful Delaware River on the Pennsylvania side, crosses back to New Jersey and then runs through wooded glades and fertile valleys with spectacular views of the countryside outside of Locktown. It is of medium difficulty going mainly from the flat river bank to the rolling hills of southern Hunterdon County. There are two steep inclines which may require some walking on the part of the novice rider, but the beauty of this ride is worth it.

Maximum round-trip distance: 40 miles
Course: rolling hills with 2 steep ones
Minimum travel time: 5 hours

Directions:

> From Lambertville, walk your bike across the bridge over the Delaware into New Hope
> Right onto Route 32 north and follow to bridge across the Delaware to Frenchtown, New Jersey--a distance of about 17 miles
> Cross the bridge into Frenchtown; take Bridge Street through the town
> Right onto Route 12 North (Kingwood Avenue) in the direction of Flemington
> Right onto Horseshoe Bend Road (just at the bottom of the steep hill)
> Right at the stop sign onto County Route 519
> First left onto unmarked Barbertown-Kingwood Station road
> Right onto unmarked Ham Road, the _first_ _right_ _after_ Muddy Run Road, which is marked

78

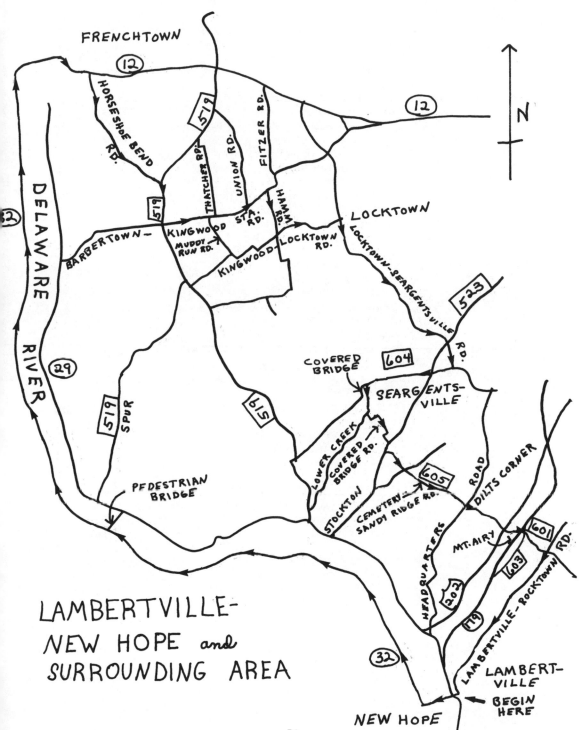

FRENCHTOWN

(12)

(12)

N

HORSESHOE BEND RD.

519

THATCHER RD.

UNION RD.

FITZER RD.

519

HAMM RD.

LOCKTOWN

DELAWARE

RIVER

(32)

(29)

BARBERTOWN—

KINGWOOD STA. RD.

MUDDY RUN RD.

KINGWOOD-LOCKTOWN RD.

LOCKTOWN-SEARGENTSVILLE RD.

523

COVERED BRIDGE

604

519 SPUR

619

SEARGENTS-VILLE

LOWER CREEK

COVERED BRIDGE RD.

605

ROAD

DILTS CORNER

PEDESTRIAN BRIDGE

STOCKTON

CEMETERY— SANDY RIDGE RD.

HEADQUARTERS

MT. AIRY

601

LAMBERTVILLE-NEW HOPE and SURROUNDING AREA

202

(79)

603

LAMBERTVILLE-ROCKTOWN RD.

(32)

LAMBERT-VILLE

BEGIN HERE

NEW HOPE

Left at the intersection onto unmarked Kingwood-Locktown Road

Right onto the Locktown-Seargentsville Road (uphill here)

Cross County Route 523 at the stop sign

Right onto County Route 604 (you will see the Delaware Township School directly in front of you), and proceed into Seargentsville

Continue through Seargentsville down the hill to the Green Seargents Covered Bridge

Left immediately before the covered bridge onto unmarked Covered Bridge Road

Bear left after you pass the sign saying "Valley Brook Farm" to stay on course (do not continue along the brook)

Right onto County Route 523

Immediate left onto unmarked Cemetery Road, which becomes Sandy Ridge-Mt. Airy Road

Left at the stop sign beside the cemetery

Immediate right, in front of the Sandy Ridge Church.

(if you wish a more direct route back to Lambertville, use the alternative below)

Go straight through Dilt's Corner and pass under Route 202

Cross Route 179 in the direction of Mt. Airy designated by a large sign

In Mt. Airy, first left beside the church at the sign saying South Hunterdon Regional High School.

After passing the high school on your right and the Circle A Ranch on your left

Right onto the Lambertville-Rocktown Road which runs behind the high school

Right at the intersection

Left at traffic light into center of Lambertville.

Alternative: In Dilt's Corner, which is a crossroads identified by a small faded sign, you may turn right onto the Lambertville-Headquarters Road, which will lead you back to New Jersey 29 onto which you will turn left to return to Lambertville. However, as of this writing, the road is in poor condition with about two miles of gravel. It is a beautiful ride otherwise with almost no traffic and lovely views.

80

PART IV: FROM CITY TO COUNTRY

Three tours from urban centers to the nearby countryside. Included are visits to the exotic Great Swamp, the lush Watchung Reservation, and the beautiful international botanical gardens of Skylands Manor. Again, it is astounding to realize how quickly even the most congested areas of New Jersey give way to rural beauty and calm.

Tour 18: Newark to the South Mountain and Watchung Reservations

This tour begins in Newark and runs through park lands in some of the finest suburbs of New Jersey. It might be thought of as a kind of hands across the trail tour uniting inner city and suburban residents. When I worked out the course, I was astounded to realize that Newark's downtown center is ony 6 miles from South Orange--communities poles apart in economic and social status. I marveled at how easy it is for inhabitants of the crowded inner city of Newark to escape to the cool serenity of the Watchungs-with a bicycle.

Although the trip begins at the train station in Newark, it is meant to serve the whole suburban area from the Oranges to Plainfield. Residents of Summit, Short Hills, Cranford, Fanwood, and so on, can easily find their way to the trail from their communities, adjusting the starting and stopping points to their needs.

The tour is also directed to the New Yorker who desires quick access to an area with a serene and wooded atmosphere--one of the reasons why it begins at the train station. The New York cyclist simply takes the PATH train across the Hudson to Newark during non-peak hours. But you must have a permit, which is easily obtained. For information call 212-432-1272 or 201-963-2677.

Maximum round-trip distance: 45 miles
Course: moderately hilly, but a few steep grades
Minimum travel time: 5 hours

Directions:

Leave the train station in Newark via Market Street
Bear left onto Springfield Avenue

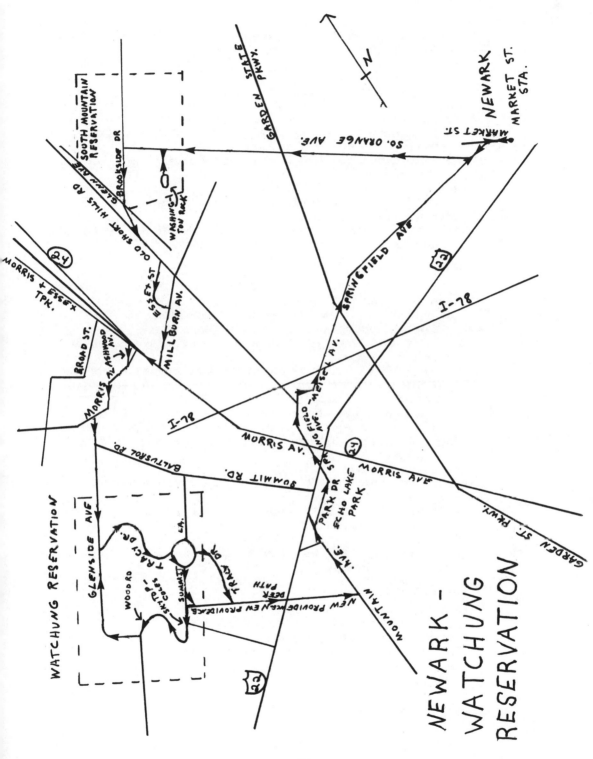

NEWARK – WATCHUNG RESERVATION

83

Right onto South Orange Avenue and proceed into South Orange

Left onto Crest Drive immediately after entering the South Mountain Reservation

Go along Crest Drive past the deer paddock and around the barrier to automobiles to Washington Rock. After enjoying the view, return to the deer paddock and go left onto Summit Trail and around to Crest Drive and again left back to South Orange Avenue

Left onto South Orange Avenue--be careful here because of heavy traffic

Left onto Brookside Drive

Cross Glenn Avenue continuing on Brookside Drive

Left onto Old Short Hills Road

Right onto Essex Street following the signs for County Route 527 (around to the left and to the right)

Follow the signs for Millburn Avenue

Right onto Millburn Avenue in Short Hills

Right at the intersection, following signs for Broad Street and Summit

Left onto Ashwood Avenue- go one short block and then

Right onto Morris Avenue

Bear left onto Glenside Avenue and into the Watchung Reservation

Left onto W.R. Tracy Drive at the sign for Lake Surprise

Right onto the traffic circle and then right again in the direction of Scotch Plains

Right onto New Providence Road

Left onto Coles Avenue, which becomes Skytop Drive (ignore the Glenside Avenue you will see to your left and continue on Skytop Drive)

Right onto Glenside Avenue

Right again onto W.R. Tracy Drive and retrace a small part of your path

Enter the traffic circle again and continue on around past the exit to Scotch Plains that you took before

Right onto the continuation of W.R. Tracy Drive

Left at the end of Tracy Drive onto Deer Path, which becomes New Providence Road

Cross Route 22 onto the continuation of New Providence Road

Left onto Mountain Avenue

Right onto Park Drive into Echo Lake Park

Left onto Springfield Avenue, which becomes Meisel Avenue and follow signs for Maplewood and Newark

Continue directly ahead across Route 24 onto Springfield Avenue

Bear right in Newark onto Market Street and back to your starting point.

Tour 19: Skylands-Ringwood Manor-Wanaque Reservoir Tour

Beginning in Paterson, which is only 14 miles from the George Washington Bridge, this tour takes you to the northeastern section of New Jersey. It is a strenuous route, but there are rewards such as the serene Wanaque Reservoir. But most beautiful is Skylands Manor with its spacious grounds and magnificent botanical gardens. Nearby is historic Ringwood Manor, another of the sites important to New Jersey's role in the Revolution.

As with the Newark-Watchung Reservation tour, this course is a study in conrasts. The poverty and shabbiness of much of Paterson quickly give way to the wealth and elegance of its suburbs.

Maximum round-trip distance: 60 miles
Course: hilly, at times steep
Minimum travel time: 8 hours

Directions:

You may reach Paterson from Interstate 80 taking the Market Street exit
Take Market Street into Paterson
Right onto Madison Avenue
Left onto Broadway
Right onto West Broadway at sign for William Paterson College. Park in the Pantry Pride parking lot on West Broadway
Continue on West Broadway to Central Avenue, cross Barber Street and go up to the steep Central Avenue hill which becomes the Hamburg Turnpike
Right onto Berdan Avenue, which runs beside the Meyer Brothers Department Store in the Haledon Shopping Center. Berdan Avenue becomes Breakneck Road.

Left onto Longhill Road

Right onto Ramapo Valley Road at the Exxon Station (Ramapo Valley Road also runs straight ahead) in the direction of Route 202.

Left onto West Oakland Avenue (after passing through the center of Oakland) following the signs for Ringwood Manor

Left at the stop sign in the direction for Ringwood Manor and Skyline Drive

Right again at sign for Ringwood Manor (up hill here to Skyline Drive-appropriately named)

Right onto Erskine Road (uphill again here)

Right onto Lakeview Avenue

Right onto Mohawk Trail

Left onto Cupsaw Avenue

Cross Skylands Road onto Cupsaw Drive

Left at the lake onto Carletondale Road

Right at the stop sign into Sloatsburg Road in the direction of Ringwood Manor

Right at the sign for Skylands Manor (1)

Return to Sloatsburg Road and turn right for Ringwood Manor (2)

Return to Sloatsburg Road bearing right to retrace your path back in the direction of Skylands

Take your first right at the Ringwood Municipal Park onto Margaret King Avenue in the direction of Warwick

Left onto Greenwood Lake Avenue (County Route 311) in the direction of the hospital (you will pass the lovely Wanaque Resevoir with its evergreens and views of the hills in the distance.

Right onto Westbrook Road

Bear left at intersection with Morsetown Road to stay on course on Westbrook Road

Left onto Otterhole Road

Bear left onto the Hamburg Turnpike in the town of Bloomingdale

Look for the Riverdale Quarry Company on your right and a colonial structure called Slater's Mill on your left--shortly thereafter

Right onto Alternate County Route 511 or Pompton/Newark Turnpike

At the traffic circle, take Route 23 south in the direction of Newark (Route 23 is busy, but has a good, wide shoulder)

At the second traffic circle, left onto Ratzer Road in the direction of Haledon-Paterson

At intersection go left and immediately right to remain on course on Ratzer Road

Right onto the Hamburg Turnpike and back into Paterson.

SKYLANDS-RINGWOOD
MANOR
WANAQUE RESERVOIR

Places of Special Interest

1. Skylands--A mansion built in the mid-1920s in the style style of an English country house with spacious grounds and spectacular gardens. Acquired by the state under the Green Acres Program, Skylands, with its magnificent international botanical garden, is a gracious addition to the park system of New Jersey.

2. Ringwood Manor and State Park--the house, consisting of 78 rooms, is a colonial structure originally owned by Robert Erskine. Later it became the property of the Cooper and Hewitt families. Ringwood was an important forge during the Revolution and today has displays of historical interest. The house is filled with colonial furniture, firearms, and household implements, and there is a blacksmith shop nearby. Food is for sale and there are ample picnic grounds.

Tour 20: The Great Swamp-Morristown-Jockey Hollow

A tour combining history and great natural beauty in an area close to urban centers. Beginning at Washington's headquarters, the course winds through the horse farms and lavish country estates of Morris County, using a combination of bicycle paths and country roads, to enter the Great Swamp National Wildlife Refuge. From there, the trail leads through Jocky Hollow where Washington's troops wintered in 1779-80 and which is now a lush, green park. This is a tour exceptional not only because of the historical significance of the places visited, but also for the almost stunning changes in the natural landscape.

Maximum round-trip distance: 30 miles
Course: Mostly flat with an occasional hill
Minimum time: 3 hours

Directions:

Morristown is located just off Interstate 287 and may be reached from New York City by taking Interstate 80 west from the George Washington bridge and Interstate 280 south to the Morristown exit. In Morristown, follow signs to Washington's Headquarters where there should be ample free parking.   If the lot is full, park in the lot of the Governor Morris Inn, which is nearby on Lindsley Drive.
Beginning at Washington's Headquarters (1), cross Morris Street
Left onto Washington Avenue
Bear left onto Madison Avenue
Right onto Old Glen Road
Left onto Woodland Avenue
Right onto the bicycle path in Loantaka Brook Reservation (2) which is easy to miss since it is a rather small opening in the fence along the side of the reservation.
Follow the bicycle path to the parking area
Cross the parking area beside the pond to the continuation of the bicycle path across the automobile road,   at the end of the path
Right onto Loantaka Way (unmarked here)
Left onto Spring Valley Road
Left onto Dickson's Mill Road

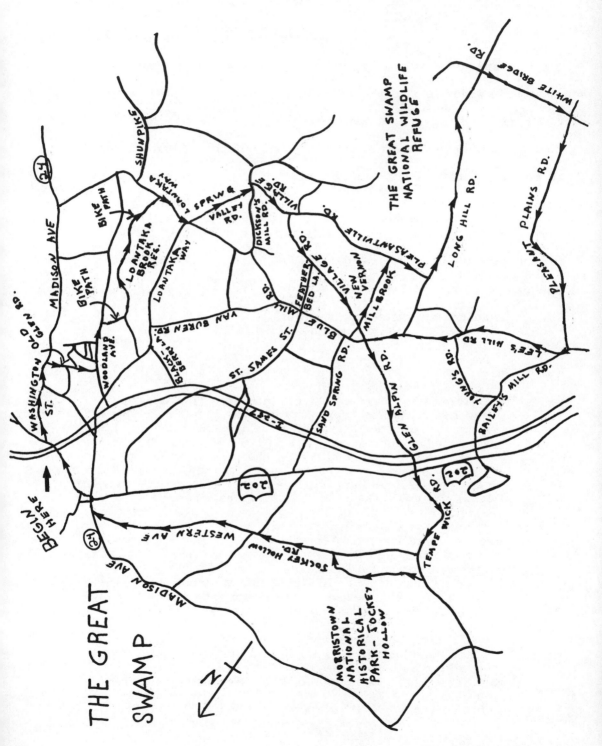

THE GREAT SWAMP

90

Immediate right onto Village Road (3) in the direction of New Vernon

Left onto Millbrook Road in New Vernon (4)

Right onto Pleasantville Road

Left onto Long Hill Road and into the Great Swamp (5)

Right onto White Bridge Road

Right onto Pleasant Plains Road back through the Great Swamp. This is an unpaved road and the pedalling will be slow, but it is worth the views and serenity of the swamp. This is less travelled than Long Hill Road. There is no alternative paved road, but the unpaved portion is only 1.2 miles in length.

Right onto Lee's Hill Road

Left onto Glen Alpin Road

Cross Route 202 onto Tempe Wick Road

Right at entrance to Jockey Hollow, Morristown National Historical Park (6) when you eventually emerge from the park

Left onto Jockey Hollow Road, which becomes Western Avenue, and continue into the center of Morristown, and following signs to Washington's Headquarters

Places of Special Interest

1. Washington's Headquarters--a beautiful colonial house, which is now a museum.

2. Loantaka Brook Reservation--lovely ponds and woods with a fine bike path much of which was opened only in 1977.

3. Village Road--notice the large estates and fine houses-- some of which you can only glimpse in the distance. Most are hidden at the end of long drives into woods and their splendor can only be imagined.

4. New Vernon--one of the few places to obtain water and refreshment on this route.

5. The Great Swamp--one of the truly remarkable sights in the Northeast. Note the waterfowl and magnificent vistas. After the woods of the Loantaka Brook Reservation and gentle landscape of Village Road, the almost tropical lushness of the Swamp in Summer is startling--as though one has been suddenly transported far to the south.

6. Jockey Hollow--the place where Washington's troops spent the terrible winter of 1779-80. Now administered by the National Park Service, demonstrations of an 18th century soldier's life are held every Saturday and Sunday in the soldiers' cabins. You may also visit the Wick House where Tempe Wick hid her horse to keep it from being requisitioned for the Continental Army.

PART V: SOUTHERN JERSEY AND THE SHORE

It is in the south that one realizes New Jersey really deserves the name "the Garden State." Here are the great farms that make the state second only to Florida and California in the production of fresh fruit and vegetables. Even though the region tends to be flat, it is anything but monotonous. The combination of shore, rolling fields, and the exotic and mysterious pine barrens make this one of the most richly varied areas of New Jersey.

Remote as the region may be in feeling, it is easily accessible to the motorist via the New Jersey Turnpike and the Garden State Parkway. It is especially close to the Camden-Philadelphia area and offers expanded oportunities to eastern Pennsylvania cyclists.

Tour 21: The Pine Barrens--Wharton State Forest

Certainly the Pine Barrens accentuate one's conscious-
ness that New Jersey is a state with a varied topography. After the
mountains, valleys, and rolling hills of the northern and central
area of the state, to see the sandy soil, flat terrain, and scrub pine
of the south is a bit like being transported from Vermont to Alabama. Riding is easy and there is a feeling of backwoods remote-
ness combined with a starkness of landscape that is usually found
only in the swamps of the deep south. While riding one day through
the area, I noticed a long, black object lying in the road directly
in my path.   I was startled to see it move and realized it was a 4-
foot-long snake--which proved to be as frightened of me as I of it.

The tour begins in the small town of Lumberton, which may
be reached from Exit 5 of the New Jersey Turnpike taking Route
451 south to Lumberton. From Philadelphia-Camden take Route 38
out of Camden to 541 south. Lumberton is surrounded by farms,
fields, and woods that to the south give way to the stark landscape
of the Pine Barrens.

Maximum round-trip distance: 70 miles
Course: mostly flat
Minimum travel time: 8 hours

Directions:

Take East Landing Street, which becomes Newbold's Corner
Road out of Lumberton in the direction of Vincentown
(surface is a bit rough and there is no shoulder, but the
road has little traffic and the fields and farms are beautiful, and the forestation lush)
Continue straight ahead at stop sign

93

Right at the intersection onto the road into Vincentown

Cross Route 206 onto Retreat Road in direction of Retreat

Cross Ridge Road and continue on Retreat Road (here the lush vegetation begins to give way to pines and sandy soil)

Just outside of Retreat at the "Y" intersection, take the right fork

Cross Route 70 in direction of Sooy Place and continue on the road to Hedger House

Right onto Route 563

Cross Route 532 in Chatsworth and continue in direction of Speedwell

Continue on Route 563 to Jenkins Neck and enter Wharton State Forest (1)

Bear right at the fork, to continue on Route 563 in the direction of Green Bank

Right onto County Route 542 (2)

Right onto Bulltown Road (just after the Bellhaven Lake Camp Ground)--road is a bit rough.

Continue on Bulltown Road to Batsto Village historic site (3)

Return to Bulltown Road and turn right onto it to continue on course

Right onto County Route 542 north

Pass through Nesco (4) and turn right at sign for Hammonton Airport

Right at the fork and then

Right onto Route 206 north--a busy road, but it has a wide shoulder and is the only road that will take you back through the Wharton State Forest (5)

Left fork onto Route 541 in the direction of Medford Lakes and Medford

Left onto Willowgrove Road

Right at the stop sign onto unmarked Atsion Road

Continue straight ahead at the next stop sign in the direction of Jackson, Berlin, and Mt. Holly at the next stop sign which marks the end of Atsion Road, left onto Tuckerton Road

Right at the stop light onto Taunton Road, which becomes Taunton Boulevard

Left onto Hartford Road (at the modernistic Medford United Methodist Church)- watch for heavy traffic here.

Cross Marlton Pike

At the stop light, continue straight ahead on Hartford Road

At the stop sign opposite Johnson's Fruit and Vegetable Stand, turn right onto unmarked Church Road (you will see the Lenape Regional High School across the road to the left)

Left onto Route 541 into Lumberton where you began.

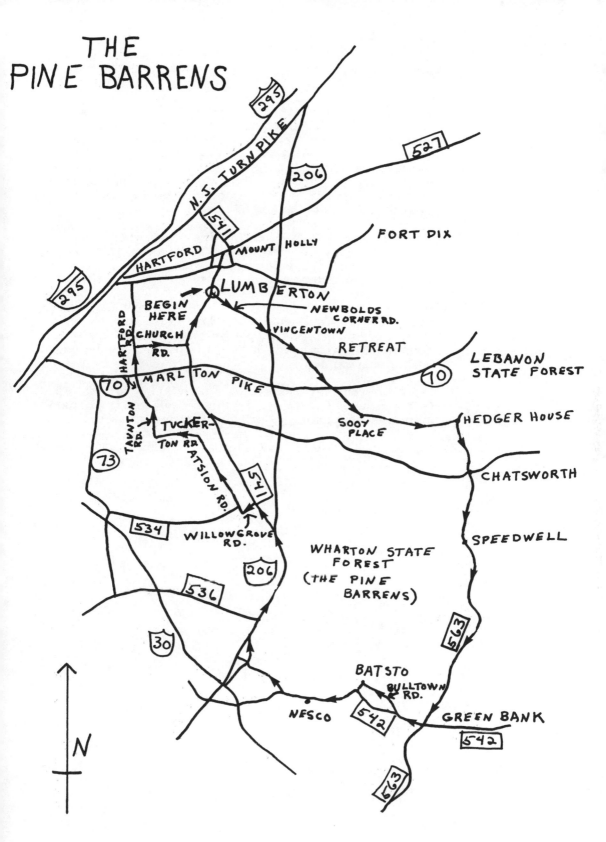

THE PINE BARRENS

Places of Special Interest

1. Wharton State Forest--the largest of New Jersey's state forests in the pine barrens. As the many town names ending in "furnace" attest, this was the center of New Jersey's iron industry, which thrived during the Revolution and the War of 1812. There are no paved roads into the wilderness area, but canoe trips may be taken through it. There are many places to rent canoes, the first of which is in Jenkins Neck.

2. Here you will see Mike's Country Store where you may get provisions. Nearby Bellhaven Lake Camp Ground is a good place for enjoying a picnic or camping out, if you are on an extended trip.

3. Batsto Village--a restored village that produced munitions for the Continental Army. There are iron furnaces, a blacksmith shop, grist mill, and the great Mansion House with its 80 foot tower that once belonged to the Wharton family.

4. In Nesco you may stock up on provisions at the Nesco Grocery Store. On Sundays, the Volunteer Fire Department serves a delicious and inexpensive breakfast.

5. Atsion Lake--fine for swimming, canoeing and camping.

Tour 22: Swedesboro to Bridgeton

A tour through historic Gloucester, Salem, and Cumberland counties. First settled in the 17th Century, the area prospered in the 18th Century and witnessed a brutal massacre by British troops during the Revolution. Its many small towns and villages thus contain much colonial architecture and other treasures of the colonial period.   The area is now the chief agricultural region of New Jersey and in the summer one sees the migrant workers toiling in the fields. A combination of gently rolling hills and flat land, the topography at times reminded me of southern Alabama and Georgia. At other times, I thought of Louisana bayou country. The overall impression is one of great open spaces and sparse population--a paradox in the most urbanized state in the union.

Maximum round-trip distance: 75 miles
Course: mostly flat
Minimum travel time: 9 hours

Directions:

> To reach Swedesboro, take exit 2 off the New Jersey Turnpike or the Swedesboro Road exit off Interstate 295. The tour begins at Trinity Church (1) on King's Highway and Church Street in Swedesboro (2)
>
> From Church Street, right onto King's Highway south
>
> Bear left in the middle of Swedesboro onto the continuation of King's Highway in the direction of Sharptown
>
> Bear right at the fork in the direction of Sharptown
>
> Continue across the intersection in the direction of Sharptown. Note the Swedesboro Tavern (3) on your right at the intersection
>
> In Sharptown, at the stop sign, cross Route 40, continuing in the direction of Salem
>
> At the Salem County Memorial Hospital, continue straight ahead onto Route 45 south into Salem (4)
>
> Left in Salem onto Broadway

SWEDESBORO
to
BRIDGETON

DELAWARE RIVER

551

N.J. TPK.

SWEDES-BORO

32-2

MULLICA HILL

GLASS-BORO

I-295

BEGIN HERE

551

N.J. TPK.

40

40

45

77

553

N

SHARPTOWN

WOODSTOWN

49

551

540

45

ALLOWAY

ALDINE

40

SALEM

581

49

640

FRIESBURG

540

HANCOCKS BRIDGE

HARMERS-VILLE

COHANSEY

LOVE LANE

CANTON

77

BRIDGETON

49

GREENWICH

DELAWARE BAY

At the second traffic light after turning onto Broadway, right onto York Street in the direction of Hancock's Bridge

After passing through Hancock's Bridge and beside Hancock House (5)

Left at the intersection in the direction of Harmersville and Canton

Continue to bear right in the direction of Harmersville and Canton

Bear right in Harmersville in the direction of Canton

Go through Canton following signs to Roadstown and Bridgeton

At the intersection where there are signs saying Othello to the right and Roadstown to the left, continue straight ahead in the direction of Greenwich (6) which you will recognize by the street named Ye Greate Street

Proceed along Ye Greate Street and then

Left onto Shepherd's Mill Road

At the intersection, continue straight ahead in the direction of Bridgeton

Cross Maple Street and continue straight ahead

At the end of Shepherd's Mill road

Left onto unmarked Fayette Street and continue into Bridgeton (7)

Right onto West Broad Street

Left onto Route 77 north (Pearl Street) in the direction of Mullica Hill

Left onto Love Lane in the direction of the Mt. Bethel Baptist Church (this turn is just beyond the Bridgeton Shopping Center)

Right at the Mt. Bethel Baptist Church in the direction of Deerfield

In Deerfield enter Route 77 north again .

Left onto County Route 540

Right at the stop light in Cohansey in the direction of Aldine

At the Friesburg intersection, continue straight ahead in the direction of Aldine

Bear left at the fork in the direction of Yorktown and Woodstown

At the intersection, continue in the direction of Woodstown

In Woodstown, take Route 45 north

Left at the sign for Swedesboro just outside of Woodstown and continue to bear right in the direction of Swedesboro

Right onto King's Highway in Swedesboro and return to Trinity Church.

Places of Special Interest

1. Trinity Church--built in 1784 by Swedish colonists and formely known as the Swedish Evangelical Lutheran Church.

2. Swedesboro--settled by Swedes from west of the Delaware around 1670 and received the name of Swedesboro about 1751.

3. Seven Star Tavern--now a private home, the tavern was built in 1762 and the small front window was used for "curb service."

4. Salem--the seat of Salem County, there are many historic buildings and houses. The town was first settled in 1675 and was the Delaware Valley's first permanent English settlement. The Alexander Grant House dates from 1721 and the John Jones Law Office built in 1736 was the first brick law office in the colonies. In addition, there is the Friends Meeting House of 1772 and many other buildings stemming from the slightly later Federal period.

5. Hancock House in Hancock's Bridge--built in 1734 by Judge William Hancock, during the Revolution the house was the scene of a massacre by the British of thirty Quakers who had supplied food to Washington's hungry army at Valley Forge.

6. Greenwich--if you continue on down quaint Ye Greate Street, you will come to the charming little red brick colonial school house. Then retrace your route back to the turn onto Shepherd's Mill Road.

7. Bridgeton--seat of Cumberland County and first settled in 1686. If you go left onto West Broad Street, you will pass the beautiful Old Broad Street Church built in 1792 with its wine glass pulpit and old whale oil lamps. In front of the Cumberland County Court House also on Broad Street is the Bridgeton Liberty Bell which was cast in 1763 in Massachusetts. Bridgeton residents purchased it by subscription and it rang out the news of the signing of the Declaration of Independence from its then location in the old court house on the Broad Street Hill.

Tour 23: Atlantic City to Cape May--"Follow the Gull"

Atlantic City possesses one of the most beautiful beaches in the world--white, wide, and sandy. Because of a confluence of islands, bays, and inlets there is always a breeze and the humidity and temperatures seem to be lower in summer than elsewhere. Because of jet travel, Atlantic City has declined in recent years from the elegant resort and rollicking convention city it once was, but with the advent of casino gambling, there is promise that its lost prominence will be recovered. Needless to say, the beaches and the ocean never lost any of their magnificence and the famous boardwalk is as impressive as ever. In September, Atlantic City is the site of a series of bike races, which are becoming more noted with each passing year. The cyclist may ride on the boardwalk at certain posted hours, which is true of all of the boardwalks and promenades down the coast. However, no one seems to mind when you ride if the walks are not crowded. The present tour does not direct you to ride on boardwalks since they are not continuous, but you may choose to ride the walks part of the way and then return to the main trail.

The course from Atlantic City to Cape May is known as the Ocean Highway and with its lightly traveled roads (most of the cars are on the Garden State Parkway) and quaint bridges, it is a cyclist's delight. As the sign says, just "Follow the Gull"--the circular markers indicating the course of the oceanside route. There is a modest toll on the bridges of ten cents to a quarter, depending

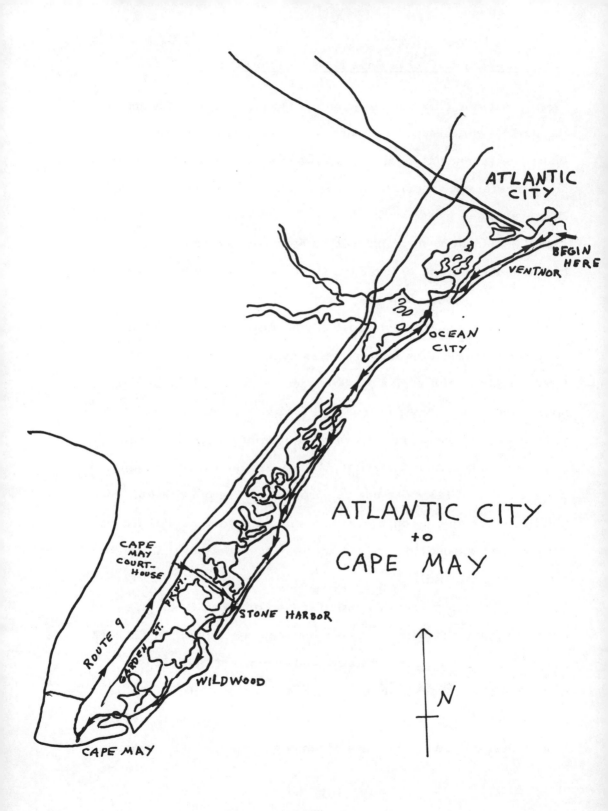

ATLANTIC CITY

BEGIN HERE

VENTNOR

OCEAN CITY

ATLANTIC CITY
to
CAPE MAY

CAPE MAY COURT-HOUSE

ROUTE 9

GARDEN ST. PKWY.

STONE HARBOR

WILDWOOD

CAPE MAY

N

on whether the toll taker decides you are a pedestrian or a vehicle. The tour passes through some suburban beach sprawl, but most of it consists of beautiful vistas of ocean, beach, and wetlands. At the end is Cape May with its fine examples of Victorian architecture and quaint streets with sidewalk cafes and curio shops.

To return, you may retrace your route back up the coast or you may take the proposed alternative up the center of the cape before returning to the Ocean Highway at Stone Harbor. If you stay in Cape May, you may want to take the Cape May Tour, which follows this one.

Maximum round trip distance: 90 miles
Course: mostly flat
Minimum travel time: 12 hours

Directions:

> Take the Atlantic City expressway to Atlantic Avenue and turn right. You may park on one of the side streets off Atlantic Avenue or even park on Atlantic Avenue in Ventnor. Wherever you park, begin your tour by going south on Atlantic Avenue, following the gull signs for the Ocean Highway. About 3 1/2 miles outside of Atlantic City, you will see a large, overhanding sign saying "Right at 29th Avenue for Ocean Drive"

> Right at 29th Avenue in the direction of Ocean City, Cape May
> Left at the sign for Ocean City, Wildwood, Cape May
> At the fork, bear left at the sign of the gull for Ocean Drive
> Cross the first of the bridges into Ocean City--here you may wish to ride on the ocean promenade to avoid the suburban sprawl
> Continue to follow the gull signs down the coast (1) to Cape May (2)

To return to Atlantic City:

> From Washington Mall, take Decatur Street away from the ocean in the direction of West Cape May

Left onto Lafayette Street

Right onto Jackson Street, which becomes Perry Street

Right at the traffic light onto Broadway in the direction of North Cape May

Right at the next traffic light onto Route 9 north and proceed to Cape May Courthouse

Right at the second traffic light in Cape May Courthouse in the direction of Stone Harbor

In Stone Harbor, left onto Third Avenue which is Ocean Drive, to cycle the remaining 30 miles back to Atlantic City.

Places of Special Interest

1. Stone Harbor Bird Sanctuary is well worth a stop. Noted for its egrets, it has many other varieties of unusual and semi-exotic birds.

2. Cape May--ecstasy for the lover of Victorian gingerbread. The beach is also beautiful and boasts a concrete promenade upon which you may ride your bike between four and ten a.m. There must be somebody who gets up that early. And, of course, you will want to stroll down Washington Mall with its shops and cafes. Note the beautiful columned portico of Convention Hall. You may wish to visit the state park and lighthouse on Cape May Point a couple of miles away. Go out Decatur Street away from the ocean, left on Lafayette Street, right on Jackson Street, which becomes Perry Street and beyond the traffic light in West Cape May becomes Sunset Boulevard. Left onto Lighthouse Avenue and continue to the lighthouse in the park, which has a fine nature preserve. You may picnic, but there is no camping in the park. There are, however, two private camp grounds in the vicinity of Cape May and five near Cape May Courthouse.

Tour 24: Cape May Tour

Cape May is a delight for the beginning cyclist or one who wishes a less strenuous course. Flat and only about eight miles at its widest point, the Cape offers a leisurely day's cycling. The cyclist can easily tour the streets of the town of Cape May without becoming lost. And the streets with their fine examples of Victorian gingerbread, quaint Washington Mall with its shops and cafes, the impressive Convention Hall, with its beautiful portico and columns are well worth exploring. This tour, however, takes you out of the town and around the Cape itself. You go north to Goshen via Cape May Courthouse and then down the west coast back to your starting point in the town of Cape May.

Maximum round-trip distance: 45 miles
Course: flat
Minimum travel time: 5 hours

Directions:

> Beginning at Washington Mall, take Decatur Street away from the ocean in the direction of West Cape May
> Left onto Lafayette Street
> Right onto Jackson Street which becomes Perry Street
> Right at the traffic light onto Broadway in the direction of North Cape May
> Right at the next traffic light onto Route 9 North* to Cape May Court House
> Left in Cape May Courthouse onto Mechanic Street in the direction of Goshen
> Right at the sign to Goshen

---

*Note: Route 9 is usually thought of as one of the most heavily travelled roads in the state, but on Cape May it is a small local road. The great volume of traffic is on the Garden State Parkway, which parallels Route 9.

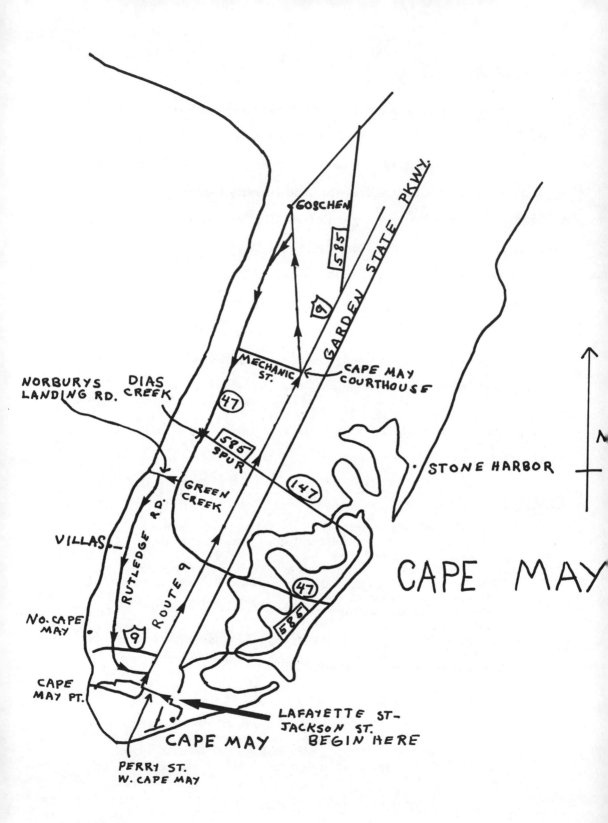

GOSCHEN

GARDEN STATE PKWY.

585

9

MECHANIC ST.

CAPE MAY COURTHOUSE

NORBURYS LANDING RD.

DIAS CREEK

47

585 SPUR

GREEN CREEK

147

STONE HARBOR

N

VILLAS

RUTLEDGE RD.

ROUTE 9

47

585

CAPE MAY

NO. CAPE MAY

9

CAPE MAY PT.

LAFAYETTE ST-
JACKSON ST.
BEGIN HERE

CAPE MAY

PERRY ST.
W. CAPE MAY

At the "Y" intersection in Goshen, make a "U" turn in the direction of North Cape May

Left onto Route 47 south

In the town of Green Creek, right at the traffic light onto Norbury's Landing Road in the direction of Villas and Fishing Creek

Bear left onto Rutledge Road in the direction of Villas

Outside of Villas, bear right at the intersection in the direction of North Cape May

After you pass the North Cape May shopping center, cross Route 9 and continue straight ahead

Bear right and around, crossing the bridge over the Cape May Canal (the same bridge you crossed earlier in getting to Route 9 north)

Continue straight ahead in the direction of West Cape May

Left at the traffic light onto Perry Street and continue back to your starting place in the town of Cape May.

PART VI: THE BEAUTIFUL NORTH -- WARREN AND SUSSEX COUNTIES

The most beautiful area of New Jersey--if you like mountains and valleys--Warren and Sussex counties are also the most difficult for the cyclist. Steep hills are a constant challenge, but the beauty of the region is worth any walking you may have to do. Easily accessible via Interstate 80, the area is, nevertheless, isolated and remote in feeling. Sparse population means light traffic on the excellent road system of these northern counties.

Almost everyone who cycles in the north has a favorite place, but all agree that there are two outstanding attractions. Old Mine Road, the oldest road in continuous use in the United States, runs along the Delaware and should be declared a national treasure. The Delaware Water Gap provides a breathtaking beauty usually associated with New England or the West. Get yourself into condition in order to enjoy the spectacular beauty of these tours.

Tour 25: New Jersey Ski Country

Unknown to many skiers, New Jersey is the site of an elaborate ski resort, Great Gorge-Vernon Valley. With its 1200 foot vertical drop, multiple lift system and powerful snowmaking equipment (capable of creating a manmade blizzard on the entire slope), this resort surpasses most of the better-known ski areas of the Poconos in Pennsylvania. The nearby Playboy Club Hotel with its luxurious accomodations, swimming pool, and restaurants adds to the variety of recreational possibilities in the area in both summer and winter. Our tour begins on the Old Quarry Road out of Hamburg, passes beside the ski resorts and parallels part of the New Jersey section of the Appalachian Trail. Of course, "ski country" for the cyclist means difficult hills, but it also means breathtaking vistas and swift, long descents into verdant valleys. To get to Hamburg, continue through Newton on Route 94 or see the back road route given in the Newton-Sussex Tour.

Maximum round-trip distance: 30 miles
Course: hilly, sometimes steep
Minimum travel time: 4 hours

Directions:

Begin the tour at the Ding Dong Dairy store (you can park in its lot) at the convergence of Routes 94 and 23 in Hamburg

Proceed south on Route 23 in the direction of Franklin

Left onto unmarked Oak Street at the First Presbyterian Church (still in Hamburg) Oak Street becomes Quarry Road, (the surface is sometimes a bit rough here)

Left at the stop sign onto Rudetown Road (County Route 517 north)

Right onto Route 94 north

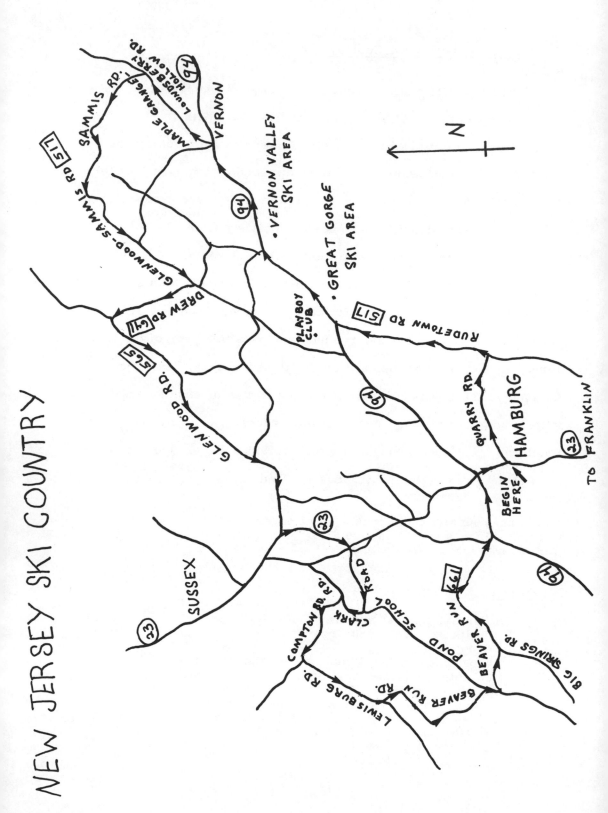

NEW JERSEY SKI COUNTRY

Left onto Maple Grange Road after you pass the ski resorts (Maple Grange Road parallels the Appalachian Trail for a bit)

Cross County Route 517 onto Loundsberry Hollow Road

Left at the stop sign onto Sammis Road

Bear right onto County Route 517 (also known as the Mcafee Glenwood Sammis Road)

Right onto Drew Road (County Route 641)

Left onto Glenwood Road (County Route 565 south)

Left onto Route 23 south (careful of the heavy traffic here; you will be on 23 for only a mile)

Right onto Pond School Road

Right onto Clark Road

Left onto Compton Road

Left onto Lewisburg Road

Left onto Beaver Run Road

Right at the intersection onto Pond School Road

Left onto Beaver Run Road (County Route 661) in the direction of Hamburg

At the Big Springs Road intersection, bear left and then right to remain on course on Route 661

Left onto Route 94, which will return you to Hamburg.

Tour 26: Hope-"Shades of Death"

A tour through the beautiful hills and valleys south of Hope. The course runs along the periphery of a fertile plain with rich, black soil, thus affording vistas of furrowed fields and waving crops, all surrounded by mountains. The region is also associated with the folklore of Warren County. Winding Shades of Death Road passes beside misty Ghost Lake. Eventually the rider enters upon Cemetery Road in this Halloween fantasy of a tour.

The trip begins in Hope in front of Hartung's General Store which is a good resting place for cyclists. The sandwiches and coffee are excellent, as is the friendly and relaxed atmosphere. Both Mr. and Mrs. Hartung are happy to fill water bottles and assist cyclists in any way they can. Hope may be reached via Interstate 80, using the Hope-Blairstown exit.

Maximum round-trip distance: 30 miles
Course: hilly, sometimes very steep
Minimum travel time: 4 hours

Directions:

Facing away from Hartung's General Store, go left down the hill of Main Street

Right at the bottom of the hill onto Great Meadow Road (opposite Millbrook Road) in the direction of the Land of Make Believe (Great Meadow Road becomes Hope Road) up hill here

Left onto unmarked Shades of Death Road, which is opposite a small ranch house about half way down the hill after you begin your descent. If the road flattens out, you have missed the turn. Climb back up the hill and turn onto Shades of Death Road. Here you will notice the fertile, black plain mentioned in the introduction--a contrast to the red soil of the surrounding area.

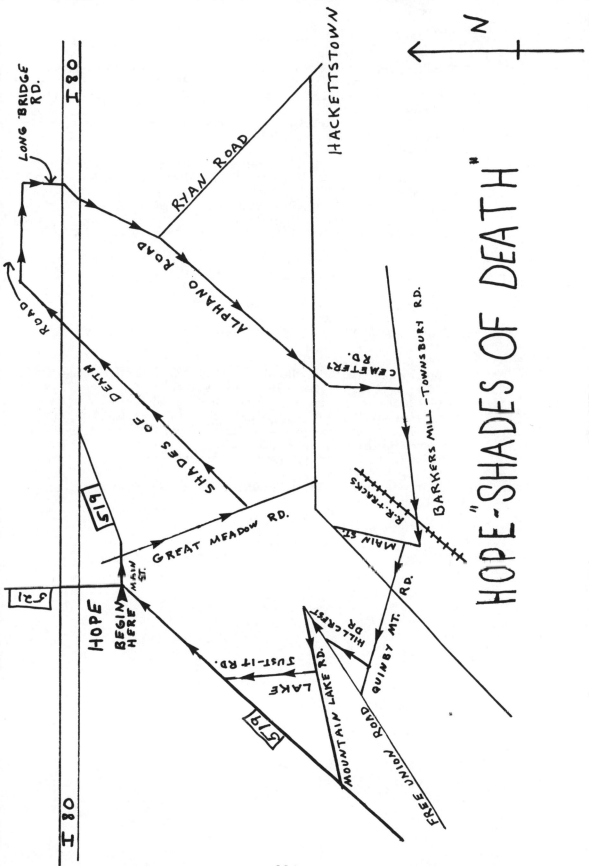

"HOPE"—SHADES OF DEATH

113

Right at the intersection where Shades of Death Road ends
 Follow the paved road around to the left as it curves

Right at the stop sign by the large red barn onto unmarked
 Longbridge Road

Right at the stop sign where you see the embankment of Interstate 80

Proceed under Interstate 80 onto Alphano Road

Bear right at the fork to continue on Alphano Road, (in other words, do not take Ryan Road--a relief since it is almost perpendicular)

Cross Route 46 onto the continuation of Alphano Road, which is now called Cemetery Road

Right onto Townsbury Road, which becomes Barker's Mill Road

Right onto Pequest Road

Go down the hill and cross the railroad track and small iron bridge

Bear right onto Main Street of Townsbury

Left at the first intersection

Cross Route 46 onto Quinby Mountain Road--very steep here

Right onto Hillcrest Drive

Right onto Free Union Road

Left onto Mountain Lake Road

Right onto Lake Just It Road--here you will see Mr. Otto Peterson's house, opposite which is a natural spring fountain whose water is delicious and refreshing, fill your bottle here. Just It Road is a remote mountain road. During the descent, the temperature feels about 10 degrees cooler

Right onto Route 519 and continue back into Hope where you began.

Tour 27: Hope-Blairstown-Swartswood Lake

Another tour through the beautiful hills and countryside of Warren and Sussex counties. The hills are sometimes steep, but the lovely vistas of Swartswood Lake and the roads through silent glens are worth the effort. As in the case of the Shades of Death trip, this tour begins in front of Hartung's General Store.

Maximum round-trip distance: 50 miles
Course: hilly
Minimum travel time: 6 hours

Directions:

Facing away from Hartung's store, turn right and cross the intersection onto High Street, which becomes Delaware Road

Right at the sign to Triple Brook Campground (the road is called Nightingale Road on some maps)

Continue straight ahead when you come to Honey Run Road and the sign for Triple Brook Camp

Proceed straight across the intersection to Knowlton Road and begin following the signs to Blairstown

At the stop sign, continue ahead onto Mt. Herman Road

Bear right as the main road curves left to remain on course to Blairstown (Mt. Herman Road becomes Cedar Lake Road and indeed you will see the lake to your left)

Bear right at the fork to remain on Cedar Lake Road, avoiding Lambert Road, which goes to the airport

Left onto Route 04

Right at the blinker light onto Bridge Street in the direction of Stillwater-Millbrook

Proceed up the hill and to the right

Left at the top of the hill onto Millbrook Road in the direction of Millbrook

Right at the sign for the Y.M.C.A. Camp about 4 miles outside of Blairstown. The road is unmarked Birch Ridge Road, which becomes Hardwick Road.

Cross the intersection and continue on Hardwick Road (surface becomes a bit rough here)

At the end of Hardwick Road, right onto Mt. Holly Road

Left onto Middleville Road (this is the first left off Mt. Holly Road)

HOPE-BLAIRSTOWN-SWARTSWOOD LAKE

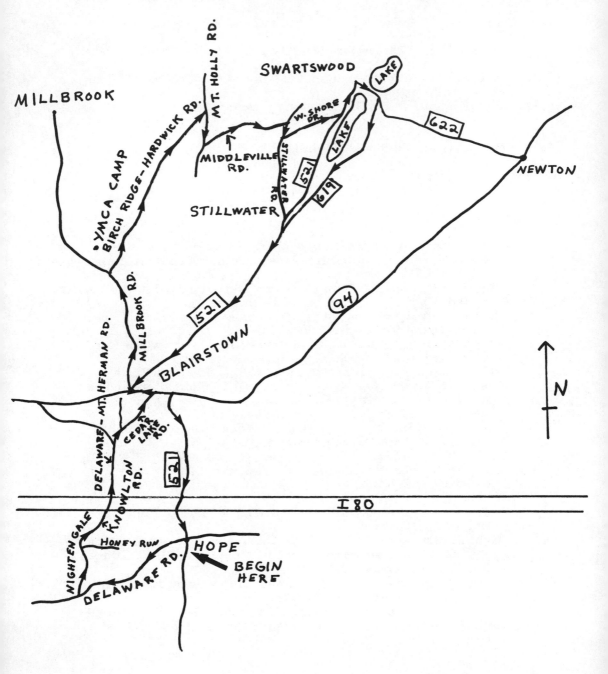

MILLBROOK

SWARTSWOOD

LAKE

622

NEWTON

MT. HOLLY RD.

BIRCH RIDGE-HARDWICK RD.

YMCA CAMP

W. SHORE DR.

LAKE

MIDDLEVILLE RD.

STILLWATER RD.

521

619

STILLWATER

MILLBROOK RD.

521

94

DELAWARE - MT. HERMAN RD.

BLAIRSTOWN

CEDAR LAKE RD.

KNOWLTON RD.

521

N

I 80

NIGHTENGALE

HONEY RUN

HOPE

BEGIN HERE

DELAWARE RD.

Cross the intersection and continue in the direction of Middleville, Swartswood

Bear right onto Stillwater Road

Left onto West Shore Drive in the direction of Swartswood and Branchville

Continue around to the left following Route 521 in the direction of Swartswood and Branchville

Right at the Texaco station onto unmarked Swartswood Road which is County Route 622. You will see the Joint Municipal Court, which occupies a former church.

Right onto County Route 619 (also called East Side Road) in the direction of Swartswood State Park

Bear right at the triangular intersection onto County Route 610 in the direction of Blairstown-Stillwater

Left onto 521 outside of Stillwater in the direction of Blairstown-Columbia

Enter Blairstown and turn left onto Route 94 in the direction of Newton

Right onto County Route 521 in the direction of Hope, Bridgeville, Hackettstown, which will return you to your starting place in Hope.

<u>Tour 28: Newton-Sussex</u>

Another tour through the farms and countryside of Sussex County. Unlike the trips in Central New Jersey, this tour offers little of historical interest, but its scenic valleys and lovely vistas are reward enough. We begin in Newton, which may be reached from Blairstown via Route 94.

Maximum round-trip distance: 30 miles
Course: rolling hills
Minimum travel time: 4 hours

<u>Directions:</u>

> Begin at the town green beside the courthouse and proceed east on the main shopping street in the direction of Sparta onto Sparta Avenue
> Left onto Hix Avenue (County Route 663)
> Right onto Route 94 north
> Bear left at the fork onto County Route 659 in the direction of Lafayette (659 is also called Lafayette Meadows Road)
> Cross Route 15 in Lafayette onto the continuation of Lafayette Meadows Road
> Right onto County Route 661 in the direction of Hamburg/Sussex (661 is also called Beaver Run Road)
> Left at the intersection onto Pond School Road in the direction of Lewisburg/Sussex*
> Left onto Clark Road
> Left onto Compton Road
> Cross Lewisburg Road onto County Route 565 south
> When Route 565 turns left, you cross the intersection and continue straight ahead onto County Route 628 (also called Newman Road)
> <u>Sharp</u> left onto Pidgeon Mill Road, which becomes Davis Road (<u>avoid</u> Haggerty Road)
> Right onto Plains Road
> Cross Route 206 onto Smith Hill Road, which becomes Blaksley Road (Smith Hill Road is unpaved gravel for one mile, but is the only way to avoid busy Route 206. If you absolutely refuse to touch gravel, go left onto 206 and right onto 94 back into Newton. However, in my opinion, it is worth a mile of walking to avoid the traffic of 206.)
> Left onto county Route 519, which will return you to Newton via Mill Street.

---

*If you are on your way to Hamburg for the ski country tour, continue straight ahead, following the signs for Hamburg.

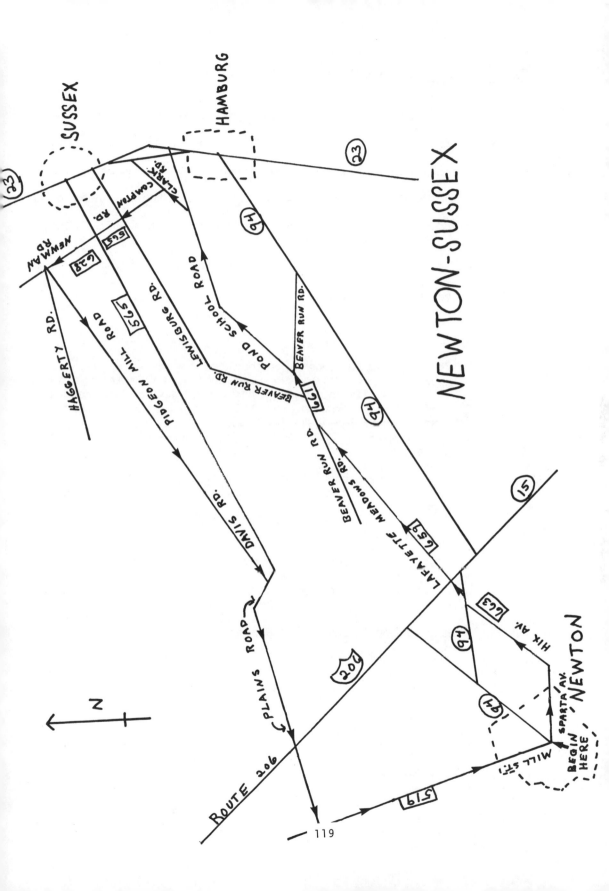

NEWTON–SUSSEX

Tour 29: The Delaware Water Gap

Possibly the most beautiful place in New Jersey, the water gap is lovely for cycling. The tour leaves from Hope, goes over the mountains to Millbrook, and then down the Delaware via the Old Mine road to the water gap. This, with the New Hope to High Point tour, is probably the most spectacular in this collection.

Maximum round-trip distance: 70 miles
Course: hilly and steep
Minimum travel time: 9 hours

Directions:

The tour leaves from Hope and goes to the water gap via Blairstown. Follow the instructions to Blairstown in the "Hope-Blairstown-Swartswood Lake" tour. But instead of turning right at the YMCA camp, continue straight ahead to Millbrook Village (1)
In Millbrook, <u>right</u> in the direction of Flatbrookville (very steep here)
Cross the small iron bridge
Right in the direction of Peter's Valley
Bear right at the intersection, passing Battali's campground (2)
Continue straight ahead to Peter's Valley (3), you are on County Route 619

(You may turn left in Peter's Valley and proceed to the Old Mine road where you will turn left onto the road. But above Battali's campground, Old Mine Road is in an advanced state of decay and is more suitable for hiking than biking. Therefore, this 3.2 mile portion of the historic road is not included in the present tour.)

In Peter's Valley, make a "U" turn and return to Battali's campground
Continue straight ahead at the camp ground
Bear left onto Old Mine Road (4)
Go through Flatbrookville and be alert for the sign to Millbrook-Stillwater
Right to recross the iron bridge and go back over the mountain to Millbrook Village (Old Mine Road forms a circle here)

Right in Millbrook Village in the direction of Water Gap and Columbia

At the end of Old Mine Road at the Kittatinny Point Recreation Area and information center

Enter Interstate 80 east for the brief ride through the water gap.*

Exit onto Route 94 for a brief distance

Bear right (opposite Stark Road) onto unmarked Warrington Road, which actually looks like the continuation of Route 94 (in other words, as 94 bears left, you continue straight ahead)

Left onto Linaberry Road

Right onto unmarked Nightingale Road when Linaberry Road ends

Left onto Delaware Road when Nightingale Road ends and follow back into Hope.

Places of Special Interest

1. Millbrook Village--a restored 19th-century village administered by the National Park Service. In the summer, there is a slide lecture and a tour of the blacksmith shop, store, hotel, church, and other buildings and artifacts central to 19th-century village life.

2. Battali's campground--Mrs. Battali is hospitable to cyclists. You may fill your water bottle from her well, whether you use her campground or not. She charges $1.50 per night to camp and furnishes hot showers and toilet facilities.

---

*It is no longer legal to ride on the Interstate in New Jersey. However, since there is no other way through the water gap at this point, state troopers should be understanding. However, if you wish to avoid I-80 when Old Mine Road ends in the Kittatinny Point Recreation Area, take I-80 west and walk your bike across the bridge. Left onto Oak Street in the village of Delaware Water Gap. Left onto Route 611 south to the pedestrian bridge in Portland, Pennsylvania. Cross the river again into Columbia, New Jersey. Follow signs for Route 94 east toward Blairstown-Newton and bear right onto Warrington Road off 94. Follow instructions above for the return to Hope. This route has a lovely view of the water gap, but is not worth the bother in my opinion since Route 611 is very narrow and has no shoulder at this point. I believe that I-80 is actually safer and there is a fine view of the gap from Linaberry Road anyway. But be careful whatever choice you make.

DELAWARE WATER GAP

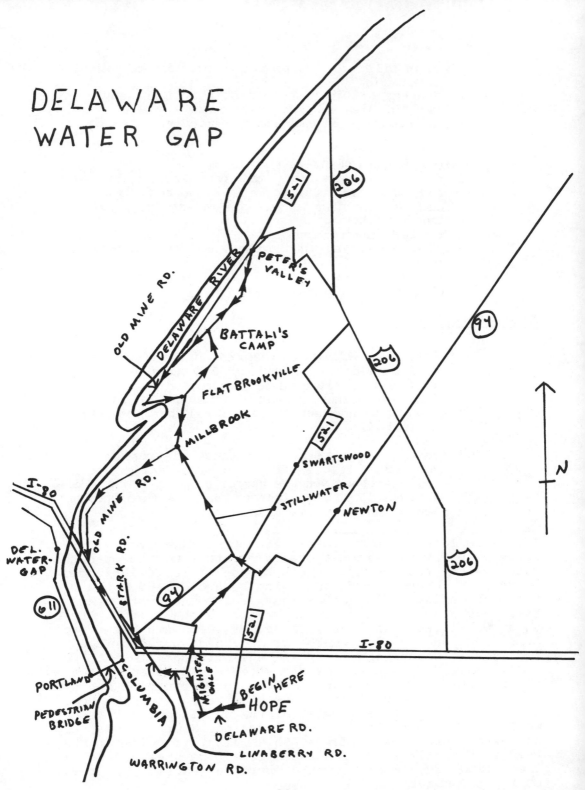

3. Peter's Valley—a craft village founded in 1970. Resident artists and craftsmen teach and ply their trade here in this beautiful and serene enviornment. You may observe them at work and buy their products in the village store.

4. Old Mine Road— originally connecting present-day Kingston on the Hudson with the Pahaquarry copper mines. First constructed around 1650, its length was 104 miles and it is considered to be the oldest road in continuous use in the United States.

Tour 30:   New Hope-Lambertville to High Point

A long tour of at least two days up the Delaware River to the highest point in New Jersey--High Point State Park. The trip begins in New Hope, Pennsylvania, crosses the Delaware back into New Jersey at Easton, Pennsylvania, and follows the river up to Belvidere, New Jersey. The course moves inland for the ride to the water gap and then follows Old Mine Road, on and off, all the way up to High Point. A difficult tour, but possibly the most beautiful and rewarding in this book, and well worth getting into condition for.

Maximum one-way distance: 125 miles
Course: hilly and steep
Minimum travel time: 2 days

Directions:

        Beginning in New Hope, Pennsylvania, take Pennsylvania Route 32 north along the Delaware River to U.S. Route 611
        Enter upon Route 611 north and continue up the river
        Right at the sign saying "Leheigh River" as you come into Easton, Pennsylvania
        Continue to follow signs for 611 north, turning right at the intersection where you see the McDonald's and the Sheraton Inn.
        Right onto the iron bridge to cross the Delaware to Phillipsburg, New Jersey (walk your bike)
        Left immediately after crossing the river onto Broad Street (you will see a sign for Alternate Route 22, which goes to the right)
        Right onto Third Street
        Left onto North Main Street (be sure you find North Main Street which is by the sign that says Memorial Parkway)
        Follow North Main Street onto River Road and proceed along the Delaware
        Right at the stop sign in Brainards in the direction of Harmony
        Left onto Garrison Road--follow as it curves to the right
        Left onto River Road again (in other words, always stay close to the river)

At the stop sign, left and under the railroad tracks, and
   right to continue along the river bank
Bear right under the railroad again and then
Left onto Foul Rift Road
Left onto the continuation of Foul Rift Road under the
   railroad again
Left at the end of Foul Rift Road onto the Phillipsburg-
   Belvidere Road (see map #2)
Right onto 5th Street in Belvidere (1)
Left onto Mansfield Street
Right onto Front Street (just past the post office)
Straight ahead onto Oxford Street and follow to the blinker
   light in Hazen
Left at the blinker light onto County Route 519
Follow 519 into Hope
In Hope, continue straight ahead onto County Route 521 in
   the direction of Blairstown (you may take a different
   route to Blairstown by consulting the Hope-Blairstown-
   Swartswood Lake tour)
Left onto Route 94
Right at the blinker light onto Bridge Street in the direc-
   tion of Millbrook
Proceed up the hill and to the right
Left at the top of the hill onto Millbrook road in the
   direction of Millbrook and follow to Millbrook Village
Right in Millbrook Village (2) in the direction of Flat-
   brookville (very steep here)
Cross the small iron bridge
Immediate left onto Old Mine Road (3)
Follow Old Mine road until you see the paved road bearing
   right (the next three miles of Old Mine road proper are
   unpaved)
Bear right, following the paved road that will run into
   County Route 619 in the direction of Peter's Valley.
   You will see Battali's Campground on your right (you
   may camp there for $1.50 per night)
When you come to Peter's Valley (4), do not follow Route
   619 as it curves to the right, but continue straight
   ahead onto the road beside the craft shop, you will see
   a sign that says "visitor parking"
At the intersection, continue straight ahead onto County
   Route 521 north (which is the continuation of the original
   Old Mine road).

Cross Route 206 and continue on Route 521 north which here
is called Tappan River Road
Right onto Weider Road (5)
Left onto Route 23 south and follow to the entrance to High
Point State Park (6)

For the return, I suggest retracing the route since no other
is more beautiful. For a different return through the
Delaware Water Gap after Milllbrook Village, see the water
gap tour.

Places of Special Interest

1. Belvidere, a fine old town with a beautiful town green.

2. Millbrook Village, a restored 19th-century village administered by the National Park Service. In the summer,
there is a slide lecture and a tour of the blacksmith
shop, store, hotel, church, and other buildings and
artifacts central to 19th-century village life.

3. Old Mine Road, originally connected present-day Kingston
on the Hudson with Pahaquarry copper mines. First constructed around 1650, its length was 104 miles and it is
considered to be the oldest road in continuous use in
the United States.

4. Peter's Valley—a craft village founded in 1970. Resident artists and craftsmen teach and ply their trade
here in this beautiful and serene enviornment. You may
observe them at work and buy their products in the
village store.

5. Stokes State Forest also has camping facilities.

6. High Point State Park—swimming and camping facilities
are available here. You may also reserve a cabin if
you write in advance to the High Point Park Administration Office, RR 4, Box 287, Sussex, New Jersey,
07461.

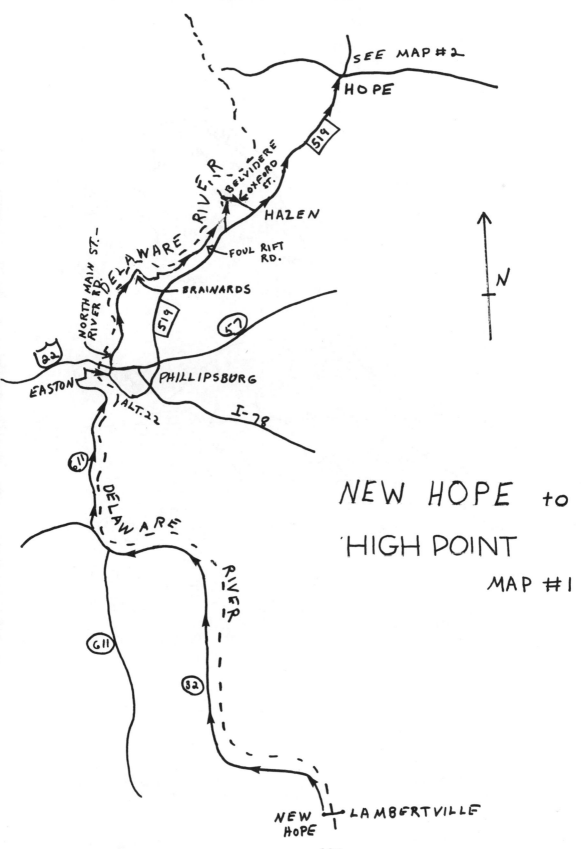

SEE MAP #2

HOPE

519

BELVIDERE & OXFORD ST.

DELAWARE RIVER

HAZEN

FOUL RIFT RD.

NORTH MAIN ST.

RIVER RD.

BRAINARDS

519

57

22

EASTON

PHILLIPSBURG

ALT. 22

I-78

611

DELAWARE

N

NEW HOPE to

HIGH POINT

MAP #1

611

RIVER

32

NEW HOPE

LAMBERTVILLE

N

PENNSYLVANIA

N.Y. STATE

CLOVE RD.

WEIDER RD.

HIGH POINT MONUMENT & STATE PARK

OLD MINE RD. (UNPAVED)

OLD MINE RD.

521

SAYTON

ROUTE 206

PETER'S VALLEY

519

STOKES STATE FOREST

BATTALI'S CAMP

MILLBROOK

DELAWARE WATER GAP, PA.

OLD MINE RD.

BLAIRSTOWN 521

206

94

HAMBURG

NEWTON

94

519

I-80

94

I-80

521

I-80

611

COLUMBIA

HOPE

611

BELVIDERE

519

HAZEN

NEW HOPE to

HIGH POINT

MAP #2